Holding on

Sue Powell

This is a true account, as near as my memory will allow, and the names of some people and places have been changed in order to protect their privacy.

This book is dedicated to Brian,

who took a leap of faith without which our dreams would have remained just that.

1. Just the beginning

It was New Year's Eve and here we were herding chickens in the pouring rain, slipping and sliding through boggy hollows, where the recent torrential rain had trashed the already muddy paths to the two chicken runs. Meanwhile, the said chickens dodged and veered in any direction but the one we wanted. Whoever it was that coined the phrase, 'It's like herding chickens', knew what they were talking about, that's all I can say! An impossible task for one, was only slightly improved when Brian joined the fray. In attempting to coax the older girls from the ditch that ran behind the garage (the most inaccessible place they could find), and the younger girls from where they were holed-up from the wind and rain, under the bushes in the front garden, and then to try steering them to their respective coops and runs, was turning into something akin to 'One Man and his Dog', except our version was more 'One Woman and her Hubby'. I snapped out commands, 'Stay there!' 'Quick, get the other side' and, 'Bloody hell Brian!' However, against all the odds, we somehow managed to steer the right chickens into the right runs within a respectable time of just ten minutes and thirty four seconds!

We were on a mission to deliver our youngest son, Sam, to our old hometown of Ledbury, two and a half hours away, and still get back in time for the New Year 'knees-up' in the village hall. Knowing that we would be back after dark, as it was already 3.50pm, we had to be sure the chickens were safe in their electrified runs before we could leave.

Sam had never taken to our move, and had been looking forward to 'living it up' with his mates at 'home' (that is, our *old* home), and escaping the dullness of his parents' new life in West Wales (not to mention the dire 'knees-up' in the village hall). Unfortunately his car had had other ideas, and within less than an hour of him setting off, the phone had rung, revealing that Sam was stranded at the side of the road. He had arrived back on the RAC recovery truck, disgruntled and well and truly fed-up. The thought of a week of grumpy twenty-something,

1

had only spurred on our decision to deliver him personally to his mates, and so the plan kicked into action.

By 10.05pm we were back in the bosom of the Welsh community and seeing in the New Year at the village hall, preparing for the obligatory tipsy midnight pecks by getting several glasses of wine on board. The night rolled on past the celebrated changeover of years and well into the early hours, with convivial chat and raucous anecdotes, until somebody decided it really was time to lock up and go home, and we were all ejected into the crisp chill of the new year, to wend our way down frosted lanes to our various abodes.

Reflecting, as one does on the threshold of a new year, we felt fortunate. We had taken on an adventure, and survived some difficult times since that day, two years earlier, when we had arrived at Nantcoed.

~

We stood on the edge of the patio, taking in the view. Three acres of neglected and overgrown ground lay before us. Swathes of brambles encroached upon tussocky pasture, and patches of reed hinted at the marshy nature of the land we were now the proud owners of. To our right, the top field rose at a steady but steep incline until it reached the boundary fence, where a magnificent, and no doubt very ancient, beech tree stood in the far corner, a protective 'body-guard' with wide outstretched branches shielding us against the ravages of the south-westerly winds. Beyond that, a neglected woodland hugged the steep hillside, bare limbs stark against the grey autumnal sky. Between the wood and the house, and running beyond the highest edge of our land, the neat sheep-trimmed grass of a meadow rose abruptly, whilst vigorous huddles of bramble and blackthorn fought for dominance on our side of the post and wire fence.

Looking down the hill, to the left of the overgrown and barely visible ditch that dissected the smallholding, the lower field fell away more gently. Alongside the lane, but separated from it by a boundary of hawthorn and hazel perched on a solid bank of stone and earth, a stream babbled its short descent to the river below.

Beyond our land, the eye could not resist being drawn to the glorious views across the Teifi Valley. The lush green fields on the far side, flanked the near vertical mountain road that led to the bleak and beautiful wilderness of the highest reaches. Nestled below, the tiny community of Felinfawr gathered around the doglegged stone bridge that linked the two halves of the village, with its stout stone church and pretty village hall on one side, and the village shop and post office on the other, where we were to find they sold an incredible array of goods in a space no bigger than most people's lounges. An eclectic mix of sheep farms, stone cottages, tasteful new builds and a short row of ex-authority houses, with a host of further properties intriguingly peppered amongst the nooks and crannies of the mountainside, combined to form the place we were now to call 'home'.

Undaunted by the task ahead of us, we naively bubbled with excitement at the prospect of taming our rundown smallholding, and relished the challenge of restoring the land to a good state, raising as much of our own food as we could in the process.

We had arrived...at long last!

~

It had been a long time in coming. I don't think anyone really thought we'd actually do it! In fact, I'm sure we had succeeded in boring everyone rigid with our 'when we move to Wales' tales for so long that we were probably regarded as 'all talk, no action pipe-dreamers'. Our friends, however, humoured us and kindly asked from time to time how the plans were going and whether the move to Wales was still on the cards. We had hung onto the dream for well over 5 years, visiting Pembrokeshire, and later Ceredigion, looking at areas we liked and marking less favourable spots in red highlighter on our AA Road Atlas. We had honed our desires and pared down the region we thought we'd like to live in, until we were absolutely sure.

Unfortunately, having decided the time was right, and having found the area we wanted to move to, we were still held back by the need to sell our house on the Herefordshire/Gloucestershire border, and with the recession

3

still biting, it looked as though it would be a long wait. It was a frustrating time, but after 8 months and a change of estate agent, we were suddenly faced with a cash buyer who wanted to complete in just 5 weeks!

Everything now went into overdrive; an online search for smallholdings, appointments arranged and a B&B booked for the coming weekend. One last check of the online property pages before we left threw up a new property we'd not seen advertised before. By some miracle it had been reduced by £50,000 that very week and now fell into our price bracket. We hastily spoke to the vendors and added it to our list of viewings before setting off for West Wales.

We arrived in Felinfawr slightly early for our 3pm appointment, having already viewed a couple of properties, one with a daunting 12 acres and a cottage that required 'some modernisation', and another close to the coast whose 'sea views' were obliterated by woodland and the neighbour's pile of rusting scrap cars. We took the opportunity to get a feel for the village, and I popped into the shop whilst Brian walked over the crooked stone bridge to inspect the fishing prospects; here is a man who knows where his priorities lie! However, on emerging from the shop I was met by the sight of Brian chatting to a chap who was walking his two dogs. It soon became evident that this chap had moved to the village a few years previous, from a place not far from where we were presently living. He was very friendly and gave us the 'lowdown' about life in Felinfawr. It sounded a great place to live. He wished us well with the viewing and we made our way up the road, to the house we'd come to see.

As we parked the car outside, we were met by the vendors, who steered us through the large white gate onto the drive, along a short, very lumpy, rock path and up to the front door. The property was a pretty stone house, painted white and with a rambling rose entwined with honeysuckle growing around the entrance. We were led into quite a gloomy hall, clad in darkly stained wood strips, with a staircase immediately in front of us and doors to left and right. The door to the right led to the library, which was small but fitted with full, floor to ceiling shelves on all the walls, and with a neat little woodburner on the wall opposite the door. The other door led to a light and airy dining room. Part way up the stairs was a brand new shower room, which managed to be modern, whilst still in keeping with the country-cottage style of the rest of the house. There were just two bedrooms, with painted wood panelling forming the internal walls. The windows were tall, making the rooms lovely and light, and the sills were low, so you could lie in bed and look at the beautiful views across open fields and rolling hills. We were in fact drawn so much to the stunning views from each window, that the detail of the bedrooms became totally lost on us. A small box room, with equally delightful views, was tucked between the two bedrooms and housed an office space.

Back on the ground floor, we made our way through the dining room with its large woodburner, exposed oak floor boards and tiny, hobbit style door to the under-stairs cupboard. From the dining room you could access the kitchen and the lounge. The kitchen was long and thin, with rustic wood panelled cupboard doors painted white, and open shelving, as well as a huge glass fronted, wall mounted cupboard which reached to the ceiling from a long freestanding cupboard below. There were two Belfast sinks, a large one with rosewood double drainer, and a smaller one at the other end of the kitchen, near the oil-fired range that sat in the centre of the outside wall. On the floor there were red quarry tiles, giving it the distinct feel of a farmhouse kitchen. At one end there was a side door onto the drive, and at the other end a door led to a small tiled passage, a boot room and a large bathroom, which housed the most sumptuous double ended bath with huge taps and shower fitting in the centre of the near side.

The lounge, however, was the real *pièce de resistance*. As you stepped down from the dining room into the lounge, you could not fail to be caught by the expansive view through the large patio doors in front of you. The whole valley lay before your eyes. Beyond the patio and gently sloping field you could see the village and the ancient stone bridge across the River Teifi. This room was a more recent addition and was blessed with a beautiful oak ceiling, supported with exquisitely crafted beams. The floor too, was polished oak, and the walls were, as they were throughout the house, painted white. Each room was further enhanced by an interesting mix of characterful, stripped wooden doors, most with latches and some with the remnants of their past existence still visible, by way of roller towel brackets or the remains of an old lock.

Outside, the fields had been sadly neglected for a few years, owing to the vendor's ill-health, and tussocks of grass grew in matted mounds all across the lower field and on the hillside, home to a multitude of voles and weasels. Behind the garage and sloping up the hill was a well planned vegetable garden with raised beds and a small greenhouse, and beyond this, almost at the top of the hill, was a small wooden chalet, which looked out across the smallholding and the valley. Nearer the house were two more outbuildings, tucked together under a relatively new corrugated iron roof, a wood store and a cold store, both with power and lighting and with a small open 'veranda' to the front and side, where logs could be stored and washing hung on wet days. I could see us living here, and inside I bubbled with excitement.

Back at the B&B, a night of talking ensued, weighing up the pros and cons and discussing what could be achieved with three acres. There followed a second viewing the next day, and the rest, as they say, is history. We had bought a smallholding! It was a few miles further east than we'd been looking, but not by far, and we just knew it was the one for us.

~

The day we moved in was, of course, momentous, and filled with a mix of emotions. At last the dream was here, but we were leaving the home we had shared for 23 years, where we had brought up our children – the first and only home they had ever known – the home we thought we'd never leave and which we had lovingly extended and moulded to our specific needs. We were also leaving family and friends and good neighbours.

The day began early with the removal men coming to collect the last of our belongings, most having been loaded the day before. Luckily the sun shone and the last few items were squeezed onto the van in the dry. Brian set off early in his truck (complete with bewildered and slightly anxious cat), as he knew he would have to stop on the way to stretch his aching back. I was left to say a last farewell to the house and lock the door for the last time. And then I was off, accompanied by our partially sedated, and deceptively named German Shepherd, Storm (who was actually a complete softie and who strongly disliked cars, even on a short journey). Somehow, although I was the last to leave, I made it to the new house first. Storm, by this time, having resisted the urge to whine *all* the way to Wales, had thankfully succumbed to the sedative and was now flaked out in the back of my RAV 4, so I even had time for a very welcome cup of tea before the van and Brian arrived.

To be fair, the removal van would have arrived sooner, if only somebody had thought to warn them about the kink in the ancient bridge. Having made good time over the initial 99.5 miles, they were met with the impossible task of getting the 40ft long lorry across the narrow, dog-legged bridge and up the hill in order to complete the final few hundred yards. After a lot of manoeuvring backwards, and a half hour detour, the removal lorry eventually climbed the narrow lane up to Nantcoed. Of course, facing uphill is not a terribly good idea if you have a van stuffed to the gunnels, as it makes opening the back doors a highly dangerous, if not fatal, operation. So there followed further adjustments, as the lorry drove up the hill until a space was found, large enough to turn in, before heading back down the hill. The ramp was lowered and we were all set to unload. Now this would have been fine, except that the lane, being narrow, meant that the removal lorry occupied the full width of the road and no traffic, not even a bicycle, could pass up or down the hill. The lane had not seemed busy on any of our previous visits, and so we felt we'd not inconvenience too many people by blocking the road for a while. However, there were two facts we were not in possession of when forming this opinion. Firstly, it turned out that we were on the lane that connected the village to the local primary school in the next village, and as a result there were two 'rush hours' to endure; one at midday when the nursery finished and one at 3.30pm when the school finished. Secondly, in order to unload all our stuff we would need to block the road for an incredible 6 hours!

To start with, when the odd car appeared, the ramp was dutifully raised and the lorry moved firstly downhill a few metres, so the car could pull into our drive, and then uphill, to allow the car to pull out of our drive. Then the lorry was repositioned outside the gate and the ramp lowered again. But it was soon evident that we would still be unloading the van a week later, if we kept this up, as new vehicles appeared within minutes of the ramp being re-lowered. So Brian was dispatched in his truck, to sit at the top of the hill, and turn back any traffic that might have hoped to travel that way. This worked, in the main, apart from one chap in a small electric car, who seemed intent on winding the removal men up by insisting that he did not have enough charge to take a detour round, but who passed us up and down the hill at least four times that day, incurring all the kerfuffle as previously described. By the time Brian reappeared, several hours later, he was frozen to the core, but incredibly knowledgeable. He had met lots of the locals, who had, amazingly, to-a-man (with the exception of Mr. Electric Car) been good-humoured about the delays to their journeys. In fact, unbeknown to us, we had created quite a stir in the village shop, and anyone who was anyone knew that we had arrived!

For the next three weeks however, I had to 'work out my notice', so I stayed with a friend in Ledbury in the week and travelled back to Felinfawr at weekends. I was incredibly busy. Brian, on the other hand, was all alone during the week, with no landline yet connected, no broadband or email and no mobile signal. In order to co-ordinate our affairs, he was forced to spend a great deal of time sat in his truck down by the village shop, which was the only place he could get a mobile signal. This lurking, quite understandably, aroused more than a little curiosity, and possibly suspicion, amongst the locals to start with, and they must have wondered what kind of undesirables they'd been landed with...well the husband anyway!

Although we spoke in the week, all be it at specific designated times, the weekends gave me a chance to catch up with who was who and what was what. Being stationed by the shop actually proved to be the ideal opportunity for Brian to meet some of the locals, and it was soon evident that this was a thriving community with lots of activities going on in the village hall. Clearly we would find plenty of excuses, should we want them, to find light relief from the hard graft of being smallholders.

In fact, within a couple of weeks, we'd had an invitation to a party at one of our neighbours' on Christmas Eve. This was quite astonishing, as we didn't know, and indeed had not even met in passing, the people hosting the party, as the invite had been popped through the door when we were out doing the supermarket shopping that Saturday.

When the evening arrived, we approached the front door with more than a little trepidation – well, it is quite scary launching yourself into a room where you know no-one, but everyone knows you (especially when your first acquaintance with the neighbourhood was to cut it off from the rest of civilisation using an 18 tonne removal van, not to mention your husband being a highly suspicious character who lurked by the shop!) Luckily, we had thought to take a bottle of wine with us as a peace-offering, which was just as well, as it appeared that everyone was expected to turn up with a plate of food to share. We didn't know it then, but this is the normal way of things in Felinfawr. All evening events start at 7.30pm (the only exception being New Year's Eve) and unless otherwise stated, everyone takes a plate of food. And a very good idea it is too, as it keeps the costs and the hassle-factor to a bare minimum for the hosts. Unfortunately, as everyone is just expected to know this, the information had completely passed us by.

However, once we'd manage to make ourselves heard above the din by knocking several times on the front door, each time at a significantly increased volume, we were welcomed inside and acquainted with our hosts, before being introduced to an ocean of smiling, and no doubt curious, faces. The place was buzzing and everyone seemed eager to meet us and find out more about where we'd come from and what we intended to do with the land. We, too, felt compelled to absorb as much information as we could about our new neighbours. As we unrealistically tried to remember names, occupations and where they lived, not to mention trying to match up respective partners (not easy when couples were split between three rooms and rarely introduced together) our brains became addled with information overload.

As we strolled home through the village and over the bridge later that evening, we compared notes and tried to recall who was who, but even as we walked the last few steps up the hill and through the gate, we were still none the wiser. It was a task which seemed far beyond our addled brains, and we retired to bed completely exhausted and befuddled by the whole experience. One thing was for sure, though, that everyone was really friendly and we were strangely feeling a part of this community right from the off.

In fact we were so accepted that we were invited to just about every function in the village hall, and there were lots! We could be out every night of the week if we really wanted; there was short mat bowls, WI, table tennis, twine & w[h]ine, jive classes, New Year's Eve party, belated WI Christmas dinner in January (as there was so much going on in December it couldn't be fitted in), Valentine's dinner, Twmpath, Cawl & Whist and various other reasons to have a good old knees-up. We decided to give the first two on the list a go; well actually Brian didn't join the WI, but he was enthusiastically informed by one of the male villagers, that the men-folk were often allowed to attend the talks, though sadly (in our informant's opinion) not the one on Victorian ladies underwear! We suspected from that point on that we were going to be in for an 'interesting' and lively social life in Felinfawr!

2. Chickens

With Christmas out of the way, and several people asking us what kind of animals we were going to keep, we felt we should at least make some kind of a start at being smallholders. One thing we were sure we were going to have was chickens, so we made this our first project.

Having searched the internet, read several books and consulted various smallholder magazines on the subject, I was reasonably confident in plumping for the Sussex as our chosen breed. They were reputed to be good layers and also good meat birds, if we decided to breed some for the freezer. The Sussex is also, very importantly, 'docile and easy to manage – ideal for the complete novice'. Using the internet (what would we do without it?) I also managed to track down a breeder close by. So we decided to go and have a look.

A lovely lady called Sandra, welcomed us and gave us a comprehensive tour of her poultry pens, and we were able to meet the five-week-old chicks that would become our laying stock. There were five Buff Sussex hens and one Light Sussex cockerel, and it was agreed that Sandra would hang onto them for us until our hen house was built and ready.

"We'll be back at the end of the month," said Brian confidently, as we left. Now, as anyone who knows Brian would tell you, speed is not a quality he is best known for. In fact, within the family, there is something we call 'Brian minutes'. These are about ten (and often a hundred or a thousand) times longer than normal minutes, and that job he said he'd do in ten minutes becomes one that takes between two hours and two days, and maybe even two weeks or two years, depending on the nature of the job. So I was very surprised by Brian's optimism.

In our past life in Gloucestershire, we had built a huge extension on our house to make more room for our growing boys, who were about 6 and 8 years old at the time. We had had help from friends, but it still took a massive 10 years to complete, and the boys were leaving home for university by then. Another example of Brian's leisurely approach was his landscaping of our garden in Gloucestershire, which was on a slope. He decided to terrace it with a wall along the 25m length of the garden, providing an upper and lower lawn. He used breeze blocks, with the intention of facing these with lovely local stone, of which he had a plentiful supply. The breeze blocks grew quickly to start with, and Brian spent evening after evening working on his walls in the fading light, reading the spirit level by 'fag light'. Then the novelty wore off and the walls stood gathering moss for the next few years, the great majority still un-faced with stone when we sold up. In fact, another wall he had started some time previous, at the front of the house, a beautiful curved wall made from old reclaimed bricks and forming one side of the entrance to our drive, remained unfinished for so long that, just as Brian had decided to make a real effort to finally complete the wall, it attracted the attention of the local police! A patrol car drew alongside Brian as he worked, and the nearside window scrolled down. One of the police officers leaned out, tutting as his eyes scanned the fresh line of bricks.

'I'm sorry sir but you can't do that,' he warned. Worried that he had fallen foul of some unbeknown planning regulation or other, Brian's heart sank. 'No,' said the officer, his mouth twitching at the corners, 'We've been using your half-finished wall as a landmark for quite some years!' Directions such as, 'Turn left just after the half finished wall', and, 'Go past the house with the half finished wall and it's the next house on the right,' it appeared, would now be a thing of the past.

So, you can understand my reservations about Brian deciding to build the hen house, and my concerns that the chickens might well be in their dotage before they ever saw Nantcoed. However, he was keen to have a go and asked me to prepare him some plans for what I wanted. I had actually seen just the hen house I wanted online. With some research as to the best height of perches, size of nest boxes and pop holes etc., and using the dimensions of the original online hen house, I was able to produce a detailed sketch of my design, with precise measurements, within a couple of days. This done, a trip to the local builder's merchants, was organised.

We knew we'd seen one somewhere in Lampeter, and when we managed to locate it again, at the end of a no-through road, it was not what we had expected. There was a large metal barn, complete with racks of wood (as you would expect), and there was an old building across the yard that looked like a three-storey town house, of which the lower floor appeared to be the shop. This was chocked full of shelves and boxes, so that it was hard to see where to find anything. And next to this, through an arch, was another almost identical room, barely 4m x 3m, with a large glass screen at one end, beyond which was the tiny office, equally packed from floor to ceiling with mounds of files and stacks of paper. We felt as if we had stepped back at least fifty years.

However, going back in time is not always a bad thing, and we were greeted with exceptional service. There were only two assistants – one, the manager I presumed, sitting at his desk in the office, and a Yorkshire chap called Rob, who luckily turned out to be an expert on hen houses, having had chickens himself, and from whom we gleaned a wealth of information, including where to get very cheap wood-shavings for bedding. Apparently, there were several sawmills in the area, where you could fill a sack for just 50p! Rob became a regular advisor over the coming weeks and months, and could always be relied upon to offer practical solutions to our construction dilemmas.

With the wood ordered and duly delivered, there followed a period of frantic activity, (alright, not 'frantic' – this was Brian we were talking about after all - but 'steady' activity) as Brian began building the frame of the hen house in the garage. Give him his due, my dear husband worked long hours in bitterly cold conditions as temperatures dipped several degrees below freezing, to meet the deadline which he himself had set. However, over time my design started to become less and less recognisable, as negotiations were entered into.

"Does it matter if this is 5cm shorter?" "Can I make the roof slope this way instead, as it would make it much easier for me, and save wood?"

Of course each alteration had an impact on the overall design, and there was a knock-on effect as to whether the door to the pop hole would still have room to be pulled up if the roof was lower, and whether it was possible to open the lid to the nest boxes if the roof was now going to overhang them. At one point I think we both felt the project was spiralling out of control, and there was a growing amount of crisis management required. The stress levels in the garage were growing, and my feet were becoming quite tender from walking on so many eggshells (no pun intended) whilst trying to cling on to as many aspects of my original design as I could.

Finally though, the deed was done and a completed chicken house, that bore *some* resemblance to the one I'd designed, stood in the garage. It may not have had the lift-off side for easy cleaning, or the slide up pop hole door, or the exact same length of perches as planned, but it looked magnificent and just like a 'real' chicken house. It stood resplendent in the centre of the garage, and, as Brian smugly pointed out, it had been completed on schedule. Amazing!

However, there was *one* problem - it was in the garage. We needed to get it onto the field and the gap between the garage and the house (the main route to the field and one of only two possible options – both of which were very narrow), turned out to be 10cm *less* than the narrowest dimension of the hen house. Not only that, but our new hen house, which had been constructed with great care to take account of the need to be able to move it easily to fresh pasture as necessary, and so was built using the lightest of materials available, turned out to weigh a ton (possibly quite literally!) We appeared to be well and truly scuppered.

That evening, after much discussion of possible solutions to our dilemma, all of which proved on closer inspection to be non-starters, and some positively ludicrous, we retired to bed with the situation weighing heavily on our minds.

The following morning though, Brian, in true 'not to be defeated' fashion, had come up with a cunning plan, that might just work. This involved a plank of wood laid across the wheelbarrow, onto which we'd lift the heaviest, nest box end, and one of us would lead from the front, using 'lifting poles' either side of the chicken house to lift, steer and pull. These 'lifting poles' were actually an integral part of the original design, so that the top of the chicken house could be lifted off the base for cleaning (as it didn't have a lift-off side) and for moving to new locations around the field. Each side of the house was fitted with two metal 'handles,' mounted vertically, so that a pole could be slid through them, rather like a Sedan chair. Brian, as the instigator of the plan, took the forward position, holding the front of the lifting poles and steering –a position of definite advantage, as he could actually see where he was going! On the other hand, I was allocated the position of 'rear gunner,' pushing the unwieldy wheelbarrow– a position with two major disadvantages: a) the whole thing was distinctly unstable, so I needed to try and balance it with the only appendage that was not already employed – my forehead - which I rested on the protruding nest box (a most uncomfortable position), and b) with my head pinned to the nest box, all I could see was my feet. If only we'd had the resources and spare manpower to film the whole procedure, we could have made a fortune on Youtube!

We wobbled our way across the pitted drive and around the side of the house to the front pedestrian gateway, leading to the front door. The drive sloped downhill and as we approached the gateway we had to make a sharp right turn, in order to line up the whole thing with the ivy-clad gateposts. Amazingly, we managed to negotiate the turn without catapulting the hen house off onto the drive, mainly as a result of increased, and somewhat painful, pressure from my forehead on the nest box as we turned. With some jiggling and manoeuvring on my part, guided by Brian shouting instructions, and with my head still pinned to the nest box and therefore unable to see anything but my wellies, we attempted to line up the wheelbarrow and its load with the narrow gap. But despite our efforts it still would not fit through. There then followed a fevered attack on the ivy growing on the two gate posts. Would the extra centimetre now available make the difference? We re-established our positions front and back and tried again, and ... yes! We were through and now bumping across the knobbly stones laid into the grass that led to the front door. But a greater hazard loomed just three metres ahead (well it would have if I could have seen anything other than my feet!). The patio steps – two of them! In a rare display of forward planning, Brian had placed two plywood boards up the steps, and amazingly we sailed up the ramp! At this point we took a breather, surprised by our good luck, and feeling pretty relieved to now be on the right side of the house. We even took a photo as proof of our ingenuity! Then we were off again, rather too fast for me at the back, it must be said. The ground now sloped down gently towards the ditch, where it then dipped severely as it crossed the ditch, before rising again up the hill to the patch I had cleared for the chicken run. The descent of the gentle slope was scary, but the sudden dip was just *too* much and the whole coop lurched forward and off the front of the wheelbarrow, landing heavily in the mud. On inspection some of the featherboard had been knocked off one side, but otherwise the hen house was still thankfully intact. We lifted it back onto the wheelbarrow for another shot, but again it slipped off. It seemed going downhill was not as easy with this system as going uphill. We decided to give in and carry the house the remaining few metres – me at the heavy end (of course) and Brian at the front.

At last the chicken house was in place, perched on the top field and looking rather grand with a wonderful view of the valley below. What lucky chickens these would be! All that remained was for the run to be prepared and the electric fence erected, and then we would at last be ready to receive our first livestock.

The weather was dreadful the next day, and with no sign of improvement. But the job needed to be done, and I worked through rain, hail, sleet and snow, cutting away the grass where the 50m length of electric netting would stand, so as to reduce the risk of any shorting. This done, I unrolled the electric fence with its integrated posts and started to erect each side of the run. As 'Murphy's Law' would have it, the integrated posts never seemed to be just where you needed them when a corner was reached, so quite a bit of adjustment was needed to get it just right, but finally the run was enclosed. All that remained was to level some of the rougher patches in the run. Of course, the chickens wouldn't have cared less how level their run was, but I wanted it to look as tidy as I could manage, and so as another squally shower of hail stones stung my face, I pulled my hood up and set about digging out the biggest tussocks and strimming the smaller ones. By the time it was all done and set up, I was totally drenched and frozen to the core (my 'waterproof' coat was so utterly sodden that it subsequently took an entire week to dry out!) I retired to the house for a hot bath, dry clothes and a seat in front of the woodburner. At last we were now ready to welcome our chickens.

The next day was cold, but at least it was dry. I was so excited to collect our chickens; I couldn't wait to see what they thought of their coop and run. On arriving home, we released our five hens and one cockerel into the coop. Leaving the door open, we expected them to be out and investigating their new home in no time at all, so we retired to the comfort of the lounge with a cup of tea, and I turned my armchair round, so that I could look out of the patio doors and watch our new arrivals. We waited with anticipation.

And waited.

And waited some more.

But there was nothing to see. Not a beak or a feather emerged. It was a real anti-climax. After about an hour of inaction, I went out to try and encourage them to indulge in some exploration of their new home, or at least to discover the whereabouts of the water drinker. Some, but not all, managed a couple of seconds of fresh air before hopping back up the ramp and into the relative warmth of the coop – it wasn't the most entertaining start.

This continued for several days and even *I* began to lose interest. My chair was turned back to its normal position, facing the television – even the inane adverts were more entertaining than the chickens.

With the chilly weather, it was easy to understand the reluctance of the chickens to venture very far, and it was to get still cooler, with the beginning of February seeing temperatures barely reaching zero during the day, and down as low as -10°C at night. Thankfully we had missed the snow that other parts of the country had had so far, though across the valley we could see the top of Felinfawr Mountain looking very seasonal with its white bonnet. This turn in the weather saw me searching the internet for answers to questions such as: How do we deal with the electric fence if we have several inches of snow? The answers ranged from: 'nothing, don't worry about it', to 'the fence will need to be dug out of the snow to prevent loss of charge. A loss of charge could allow a fox to scale the fence with ease!' There then followed several unsettled nights, where I awoke in the early hours worrying about whether or not we'd had snow, and if my chickens would still be there come the morning. However, we didn't have snow, and my worries were unfounded.

I made no secret of my lack of experience with keeping chickens, and Sandra, our chicken supplier, was exceptionally helpful in answering many of my questions, from the best types of feeder and where to position them, to how to ensure the flock were protected from red spider mite and the cheapest place to buy the appropriate medication. She also suggested scattering a handful of mixed corn in the run in the afternoon to encourage the birds out into the open, and to help them through the exceptionally cold weather we had been experiencing. As the birds were still quite young at twelve weeks, I was worried they might struggle in temperatures of -10°C and below.

The chickens had settled into a routine of coming out to stretch their legs just before dark, having a bit of a mooch about, and then suddenly all scrambling for the coop, in an effort to 'bagsy' the best roosts. These seemed to be the nest boxes, where they would all try to squeeze into one, trying not to be the one nearest to the coop wall. Of course as the birds grew this became less possible, and as the month went on it became necessary to occupy both nest boxes in order to accommodate everyone.

All the literature on keeping poultry seemed to imply that the birds should roost on the perches, and be positively discouraged from using the nest boxes to roost. The consensus appeared to be that if you position the perches higher than the nest boxes, the birds do not roost in the nest boxes. This is based on chicken hierarchy and pecking order, with the top chicken choosing the highest roost. To prevent bullying and jostling for dominance, one is advised to make all the perches the same height (which we did). This is all well and good, but my birds had obviously not read the books. However, I decided not to worry about it too much. As they got older and the weather warmer, the birds would probably use the perches in preference to the boxes and my lot would start to conform to the norm. If it didn't right itself, I supposed I might have to come up with a Plan B.

Of course, before long, we felt we really should name each of our flock (as they were going to be long-term residents, as opposed to table-birds). The experts' advice reads: 'watch your birds and identify their characters before you choose their names'. That's a bit tricky if your brood are couch-potatoes, like their home comforts and don't come out very often. However, as the cockerel was getting bigger and developing the most extraordinarily long legs, we found ourselves inspired. He strutted about with exaggerated steps, not quite 'Ministry of Silly Walks' stuff, but with an equally unnatural air. He also suddenly took it into his mind to run up to the other birds, stretch his neck out and 'eyeball' them, looking them straight between the eyes, beak to beak, before backing off and continuing as though nothing out of the ordinary had occurred, pecking the ground as he had done a few seconds earlier. This behaviour likened him, in our eyes anyway, to the eccentric dancer, Louie Spence, who with his V shaped hairline and pointy nose seemed to take on an air of cockerel-like proportions. And so our cockerel duly became known as Spence.

Having started the naming process, we were spurred on to name the girls over the following few days. We had Alice, an extremely friendly chicken who often came up to me when I was in the run and liked to be your best friend. She was named after a young lady who I used to teach in my previous life – a lovely girl, liked by everyone. Next we had Maisie, who was light amber in colour, and Flossie who was the palest blondishamber colour and was very fluffy like candy floss. She also seemed to struggle to keep her coiffure fully in order, and was often spotted with stray feathers sticking out at unnatural angles, looking as though she had just fallen out of bed after a particularly rough night. Then we had the two darker auburn chickens. They were a week younger than the others and of a neater, more compact body form. Meg was named after another ex-pupil of mine, who at the age of 8 had the most gorgeous long auburn hair (that's the pupil, not the chicken). And finally there was Pippi, or Pip, who had freckles of black across her back, and who was named after the fictional character Pippi Longstocking, who also had an abundance of freckles.

Having named our chickens, I now somehow felt even *more* responsible for them. My main concern was still the fox, and this was not helped by several sightings by Brian, and some locals, in the fields bordering our land. Of course we had the electric netting and I regularly checked it with a walk around the perimeter every few days. Our energiser (which gives the pulse to the fence) had a green light that flashed, which was great for an ageing and paranoid new chicken keeper, because when I got up for the loo in the middle of the night I could peep out of the bedroom window and check that the fence was still working.

Another advantage of an electric fence, as opposed to allowing our chickens to free-range, was that on the odd occasion when we were out all day and home after dark, our chickens were protected. This meant that we were not as tied as we might have otherwise been, which I know others who keep chickens often feel. Of course this is only true when your fence is actually working.

Being new to electric fences, and with an absence of any useful instructions enclosed with our purchase, I did not fully understand the significance when the green light stopped flashing and became a static green light, but I suspected the possible implications - essentially that the chickens might no longer be safe. I rang the company I had purchased the fence and energiser from, who were most helpful in suggesting possible causes.

"No, it couldn't be the battery," I said, as I had charged it just a few days ago.

There was nothing else to do but return the energiser to the manufacturer to be tested, as there must be a fault. As it had a 2 year guarantee and was barely one month old, they would provide me with the loan of another energiser. This came by courier the next day, and the faulty one collected. The loaned energiser, which was a different model to my own, also arrived without instructions and so I was still at a loss to understand what the sequence of lights were trying to tell me. This one flashed red and green alternately when attached to the fence – very pretty, but probably not quite what was needed. However, overnight the lights faded entirely and by morning the energiser looked completely dead.

Even I knew this wasn't right, and I set off on a quest to find a friendly garage mechanic who could test my battery. This confirmed that the battery was indeed flat, leaving only one possible conclusion – the battery charger was faulty. What a fool I felt. However, having bought a new charger, and after two days charging, all was back to normal again, thank goodness.

A few days later I was unsurprised when my energiser was returned with a note – 'no fault found'.

3. Dot

Now that we had our laying chickens named and established, if not actually laying as yet, we could start to think about our next arrivals – ducks. These were to be bred for the table and definitely _not_ pets. Brian felt he would be able to do 'the dreaded deed', and I felt I could eat them, as long as we remained business-like and didn't get too personally involved in their individual lives! We had been warned by more than one well-meaning friend that when it came to it, they felt sure we wouldn't be able to go through with the butchering. Indeed, we knew of more than one friend and neighbour who had acquired a pet duck or turkey, as the unintentional result of falling at the last hurdle.

Decision made, I reckoned that I had better be responsible for building the accommodation this time. I didn't think my nerves would stand another dose of Brian stressing over my carefully drawn out plans in the garage, and anyway, this way, I should get exactly what I intended, and have only myself to blame if I didn't. Just to make things that bit more challenging though, I chose to make it for little or no cost, by using wood from the local tip, where we discovered that you were allowed to take as much wood as you wanted. Designed around a wooden pallet as the base, I also wanted to be able to take the front off for ease of cleaning. Unlike the hen house, afore mentioned, it didn't matter how heavy the duck house was, as, with luck, it shouldn't need to be moved. Looking at my plans, it was clear that I was going to need several wooden pallets, if I was to have enough _free_ wood to complete the job.

I managed to beg a couple of free pallets from the local builders' merchant, and scavenged another couple from the tip. Using pallets however, was not an easy option, as extracting the useable wood involved a lengthy dismantling process with a crowbar and the removal of a mountain of rusty nails, some of which were stubbornly reluctant to yield to brute force. This slowed me down considerably. Some pallets were easier than others to pull apart, but most were frustratingly difficult. In an effort not to fall foul of the same problem we'd had with the completed chicken house, I decided to build the duck house in-situ. Although this involved an inordinate amount of walking back and forth from the field to the garage (where the electric saw was located) it did avoid the ridiculous palaver of manoeuvring the finished item onto the field - and this construction was likely to be even heavier than the first!

With the help of some featherboards for the roof, which we *did* purchase, the duck house was completed for just a few pounds. This was a much more frugal solution than the chicken coop, that had come in well over budget at £250! That was an awful lot of eggs required before costs would be recouped, and probably not as cost effective an option as we had initially anticipated. With a lick of paint (courtesy of a tin left over from some previous project) we were soon ready to receive our ducks.

It was whilst I was completing the paintwork on the duck house, that I heard what I thought was someone cutting trees down in the wood above us. However, as it turned out it wasn't a chain-saw I'd heard, but hundreds (and I mean *hundreds*!) of frogs in our two small ponds. On closer inspection, the ponds were positively bubbling with frogs. Surely it was far too early for frogspawn? All my books said that frogs generally paired up in March or April, but we were still only just into February, though the weather had been warmer of late, even reaching the dizzy heights of 10°C at times. This must, we supposed, have spurred the frogs into action. However, hard frosts were predicted for the coming few days and one wondered how the frogspawn would fair. With nothing but cold and wet conditions since our arrival in Felinfawr, one couldn't help but wonder if this slightly warmer weather we'd had was as good as it got in the west of Wales, and maybe the frogs were just making the most of this one and only window of opportunity! Anyway, fortunately, the weatherman was wrong and the frogs were vindicated, with the mild spell set to remain for at least a few more days.

By mid-February, we were becoming creatures of habit and a routine of chores established itself. We were usually up by

9am and ready for action by 10am. I told myself that this would change in the summer when the sun would tempt us to leave the warmth of our bed much earlier, but I was not entirely convinced. Having made it to the kitchen for a simple breakfast, we generally worked outside on our individual projects until 2pm, when we would re-group for lunch. Then we were out again, more or less whatever the weather, until around 6pm, when it was too dark to see what we were doing and we'd admit defeat and retire wearily to the house, light a fire, have some tea and put our feet up for the night, nursing the aches and pains we had gained during the day.

It was on a night such as this, just as dusk was falling, when Brian and I were both tidying up after the day's work, that we heard our cat, Dot, issuing a long drawl of vociferous expletives somewhere near the woodshed. This may have been directed towards one of the feral cats we'd previously seen in the area, or possibly even a fox. We called her, but there was no reply. We stalked in and around the woodshed trying to catch sight of her in the rapidly diminishing light (which is not easy when you are looking for a mainly black cat). She seemed to have completely disappeared. Just as we were wondering where to look next, plaintiff cries reached us from the canopy of the ash tree which stood high on the bank behind the woodshed. The trunk was long and straight, with no lower branches whatsoever by which she could descend - it appeared that she was well and truly stuck. My heart sank; I had been looking forward to putting my feet up in front of the woodburner, and I did not relish the thought of climbing to some stupidly excessive (and very scary) height, especially since the cold weather had returned and its icy chill was nipping hard at our fingers and noses. I was not even sure our triple-extending ladder would be long enough! Brian is not good with heights, and can get vertigo just thinking about climbing onto the first rung of a stepladder, so I knew it would be down to me to make the ascent. A swirl of nausea swept the pit of my stomach.

Just getting to the tree in question was not easy. It was now pitch-dark and we had to negotiate the slippery bank above the old well by torchlight, hanging onto saplings to pull ourselves up. Four further saplings then had to be pruned from the base of the ash tree, before we had any chance of getting the ladder close enough to the trunk. The tree was also growing uncomfortably close to a barbed-wire fence. Eventually though, we managed to position the ladder firmly against the trunk and extend it to its full height. Unfortunately, this still left us short of where the cat was by over a metre, but, urged on by her pitiful cries, we had little choice but to try and reach her. And so I recklessly launched my rescue mission and climbed the ladder. Standing as close to the top of the ladder as I dared, I stretched my left hand up and just managed to touch Dot's front paws. I was not near enough; I would have to go even higher! I took another step up and wrapping my right arm around the only branch within reach, and with my knees picking this moment to start quivering uncontrollably, I managed to grab the scruff of her neck with my left hand. A lot of very unpleasant feline swearing and growling followed, and I just hoped she wouldn't scratch me, as I would surely have to drop her if she did. I had my own problems to deal with – namely that with my right arm wrapped around the branch, and the cat occupying my left hand, I didn't have a spare hand with which to grab the top of the ladder some distance below, level with my knees. One thing was clear, I couldn't stay there all night, and it was getting noticeably colder, so I bravely (and probably somewhat foolishly) let go of the branch and slowly reached down with my right hand until I could feel the top of the ladder. The cat being suspended from my extended left hand, necessitated a one-handed descent, though I discovered that by leaning my body against the ladder I could steady myself a little. My hands were shaking and my knees were like jelly, so that every step down caused the ladder to bounce back and forth alarmingly. When my feet (and the cat's) at last reached *terra-firma*, I breathed a huge sigh of relief. It is not an experience I ever wish to repeat. Of course, we then had to manoeuvre the cumbersome ladder back down the slippery bank in the dark – a task not made any easier when your knees feel weak and you appear to have all the strength and stability of an India rubber man, but our mission was accomplished all the same.

This was not the first scrape Dot had found herself in since our arrival in Felinfawr. Soon after we'd erected the electric fence for the chickens, Dot felt compelled to get a closer look at the strange feathery things that had appeared in the middle of her best hunting patch. Agile and athletic as ever, she tackled the fence as she had done every other fence she'd climbed, by launching herself at it, and then scrambling over the top. Only this time of course the experience was embellished with an electric shock! We were in the lounge at the time and caught sight of a demented black shape dropping into the chicken pen and then bouncing around it like a pinball. We quickly realised what had happened and I made a bee-line for my wellies. But before I could get out there, Dot, feeling trapped and obviously in tremendous peril, from both the fence and the 'strange feathery things', had scaled the fence again on the far side and made her escape – enduring a further electric shock in the process!

There then followed a period of dignified sulking in the privacy of the bramble patch further up the hill, whilst she tried to get her head around what had just happened and gather herself together away from prying eyes. Eventually though, after a suitable period of time, calculated to ensure that all witnesses to the humiliating ordeal had wiped it from their memories, she allowed herself to be coaxed out of her sanctuary, and accepting the invitation to relax in the lounge, she strolled through the patio doors with head and tail held high and a nonchalance that *almost* covered her embarrassment. So effective was her performance that we might well have been duped into thinking we'd imagined the whole incident, except for the fact that the hairs on her tail stood out like a bottle-brush, giving the game away somewhat.

~

The last weekend in February finally saw a spell of much needed sunshine. This improvement in the weather happily coincided with a visit from our eldest son, Jack, and his girlfriend, Ellie. Jack, never one to sit still for too long, decided to help us build the duck run over the weekend. When he'd offered however, he hadn't banked on Brian dragging him up to the Community Woodland to help him fell the wood for the job before he could even start. The woodland, just half a mile up the hill behind us, was having one of their 'thinning out' days, whereby you paid a tenner and were allowed to take whatever wood you could cut with a handsaw. We needed about fourteen eight-foot stakes, and so off they went, armed with a selection of saws and garden clippers. It was a task that was to take most of the day, so Ellie and I headed off to the coast to chill out on the beach with a picnic, followed by a visit to the best ice-cream parlour in Cardigan Bay. We didn't feel guilty at all, knowing the boys were working hard! However, the next day saw 'all hands on deck' as we started the main job.

I was given the task of stripping! Removing the bark from the posts with a draw-knife was a skill we had picked up on one of our volunteering days up at the wood. Jack took on the job of digging the two-foot deep holes for the posts and, with Ellie's help, sinking the posts three feet apart. This was not an easy job, as much of the ground was heavy blue-clay and very stony. In order to keep the posts firm and sturdy, the holes had to be filled with stones, tamped down around the posts with a strong pole, and then filled with clay and firmed with the foot. It was slow going and frustratingly the job could not quite be completed before Jack and Ellie had to leave for home. Brian and I had to complete the job. Well, we sank the remaining two posts in the holes that Jack had dug for us and completed the rails at the top of the frame, before Brian found more important things to do, like chopping up wood, and I was left to finish the job on my own – some just don't have the staying power.

Luckily our youngest son, Sam, decided he would come home from uni for a few days, to work on his car, and I hoped I might get some help from him to finish the run. Of course going to fetch him from Swansea Uni held up progress, as did driving to Aberystwyth the following day, for a part he needed (Sam's car being off the road whilst repairs were on-going). However, in between running my taxi service, I managed to secure a row of fine black plastic mesh all the way around the bottom of the frame, digging it into the ground where necessary due to the slope of the land. Ducks are not the brightest of creatures, despite their adorability, and when faced with a fox on the outside of their run they are inclined to respond by jabbing their heads through the wire in a misguided attempt to ward off the predator. We had experienced this in the past, when we'd kept a few call-ducks in Gloucestershire. Admittedly the duck in question had had ducklings at the time, and she was probably defending her babies, being the excellent mother she was, but the result was very distressing - a broken beak, snapped as the fox clawed at the wire. She unfortunately had to be put out of her misery, as the damage was irreparable and she must have been in incredible pain.

So the black mesh was a vital component in the design of this run, and with it in place, I was ready to somehow put the wire netting on. When we had discussed tactics for this a few days earlier, Brian and I had decided this was definitely a two person (if not three person) job. Now, left to finish the job alone, it seemed to have become a one person job!

Unrolling wire netting and hammering staples to it, whilst keeping it taut, is no easy task for one, especially when up a stepladder that insists on sinking into the soft ground and leaning precariously, but I managed to complete the job pretty much single-handedly, with only a little help from Sam when it came to a couple of spots on the roof. With a door put together from 2" x 1" wood strip the duck run was complete, and the finished pen was a real masterpiece, in my opinion.

The breed of duck we opted for was the Cherry Valley – a breed a little smaller than an Aylesbury, but bred specifically for its meat. Cherry Valley is actually a supplier of ducks for Chinese cuisine, so I guessed this must be a good meat bird. I had also read about it in the 'Smallholder' magazine. Now I just had to find some. Having scoured the internet for breeders, it became obvious that live birds would cost us too much. We had to produce our meat at a price lower than that we'd pay in the shops – otherwise what was the point? I then hit on the idea of buying some hatching eggs at just £1.10 each. We had hatched call-ducks in the past, and so incubating eggs held no fear for us. I had bought a lovely new, all singing, all dancing incubator some months before we'd moved, in preparation for our new life as smallholders, for just this sort of eventuality. Ducks are known for being tricky to incubate artificially, as the levels of humidity they need are critical, but our new incubator was digitally controlled and maintained the temperature and humidity all by itself. The humidity level was ingeniously achieved by way of a little pump attachment that regularly pumped small amounts of water from a jar, through a tiny plastic tube into the incubator and onto something rather like blotting paper. This was a definite step forward and a huge improvement on our old incubator, which had involved a huge amount of guesswork, a humidity gauge and a thermometer, both of which had the teeniest-tiniest increments, that those of us with older eyes had little or no chance of reading with any degree of accuracy, even with the aid of glasses. And anyway, by the time we *had* read them, the temperature had fallen and we still had no idea what it had been before we'd lifted the lid off the incubator to read it! With the new incubator, the temperature and humidity could be set automatically and was displayed in large red and green digital figures on the lid, so we could check whenever passing (even in the dark) that all was as it should be. We set the incubator up in the dining room a few days prior to the expected arrival of the eggs, so we could feel confident with the operation of this high-tech piece of kit.

Then, one morning, Martin, the postman, knocked on the front door with a parcel for us. It was our duck eggs, sent by first class post, encased in a purpose-built polystyrene cube wrapped in masses of parcel tape; one dozen large, pure white eggs. As recommended, I placed these pointed end down between the plastic rails of the incubator, making sure the eggs were all held as tight as possible, but without excessive pressure. I then replaced the lid and left the incubator to re-establish the temperature and humidity that I had set (37.5°C and 59% humidity). This incubator would even turn the eggs for me too, rocking the eggs one way and then the other several times a day. Amazing! I marked the date on the calendar and counted forward 28 days, noting the estimated hatching day. Everything was prepared and ready for the ducks, but there would be plenty of other jobs to occupy us over the coming weeks, and several unforeseen challenges to test our mettle.

4. Spring

March started with some beautifully warm sunny weather, but within just 4 days the temperature had dropped and a cold wind whipped down the valley, bringing some heavy hail storms, which left a thick covering of small balls of ice across the garden. There was even excitement amongst the chickens, who, thinking this was some kind of new-fangled layers' pellet, were tempted out of their coop to taste the strange icy stuff.

Brian, being generally grumpy at the slightest hint of anything cold or wet in the way of weather, had a less positive reaction to the icy stuff. After dark, and following yet another heavy fall of hail, Brian ventured out to check the slug trap that he'd set amongst his raised beds in the vegetable garden. He'd had a lot of trouble with slugs attacking the tops of his newly planted shallots and had sunk a small bowl of beer into the ground, which the previous evening had netted a considerable number of the slimy villains. Checking the slug trap had become an after-dinner ritual that Brian relished, as he took his scissors to the unfortunate creatures, in revenge for the damage caused to his beloved shallots.

On this particular evening, Brian disappeared as usual with scissors and torch in hand, to wage war in the vegetable patch. However, when he reappeared in the lounge doorway a few minutes later, it was a bewildered and rather dishevelled Brian that stood before me. I scanned the forlorn figure and as my eye swept from face to foot I could not help but to alight on two wet muddy circles that now adorned the knees of my husband's jeans.

"What happened to you?" I asked, trying to imagine what manner of mishap could possibly have occurred within the short distance between the back door and the vegetable plot.

"Well... I stood on the path and leaned over to check the slugs, as I usually do," he started, "And as I stood there I felt my feet, ever so slowly, slide backwards on the hailstones."

"So, if it was that slow, why didn't you stop yourself?" I asked (it seemed the obvious question).

"What with?" came his exasperated reply, his voice having risen by at least an octave. "I had the torch in one hand, and my other hand was holding onto the side of the raised bed!"

With no hope of solving his dilemma in the short time available, he had resigned himself to his fate and slipped slowly backwards, gracefully allowing his legs to be taken to full stretch before, inevitably, collapsing to his knees on the mud path. This recurring image replayed in my mind all evening and kept me chuckling for quite some time after (and actually, still brings a smile to my face even now).

Luckily the weather improved slightly over the following few days and we saw more of the sun, though it remained pretty chilly in the wind, but there was no more hail to cause further shenanigans in the vegetable garden, thank goodness. In fact, spring was very definitely in the air. The welsh mountain sheep in the fields that surrounded us were busy producing lambs left, right and centre, and the farmer's lad was constantly up and down the lane on his quad bike, checking on progress.

Nature was kicking into action wherever you looked. Whilst sitting in the car on the drive, waiting for Brian as he locked the back door, prior to our weekly shopping trip, I spotted a little wren visiting one of the rope nest 'boxes' that the previous owners had slung under the eaves of the wood shed. She (well, I'm sorry, but it had to be a 'she' with the patience and care she was exhibiting) was selecting dead leaves from the hedgerow at the side of the drive, and taking them to the nest, where she spent some time arranging them 'just so'. However, on at least half her journeys back to the nest, she managed to drop the carefully chosen leaf and had to return to the hedgerow to find another. Her perseverance was admirable. She worked relentlessly, despite her difficulties and undoubted frustration, where lesser souls might have been tempted to say 'Sod it!' and flounced off in a dark mood. It was a truly inspiring sight.

Another thing we noticed around this time, was the tendency for the blue-tits to hang about the wing mirrors of our vehicles, seemingly unable to resist the temptation to check themselves out. Of course the explanation for this behaviour was, in truth, more to do with the males warning off intruders to their

31

territory, particularly with the breeding season imminent. Unfortunately these cocky little birds, who, let's face it, are renowned for their intelligence when it comes to pinching the cream from the top of milk bottles (back in the day when the milkman actually delivered it to your doorstep, and in bottles) let themselves down rather when it comes to recognising the image in the mirror as their own. The activity also seemed to necessitate the production of a considerable quantity of white droppings, creating vertical 'go faster stripes' on the dark grey paintwork of our RAV 4, which helped to distinguish us from all the other dark grey vehicles on the road, making us instantly recognisable, but for all the wrong reasons.

We had exerted a great deal of time and energy building coops and pens that afforded our birds the best protection we could give them from the dreaded fox, but it was still disconcerting one morning, to be awoken at first light by the squeals of two (yes two!) foxes. On rushing to the bedroom window, still half asleep and unsure of what could be creating such a strange noise, I thought I saw (without my contact lenses in, to be fair) two cocker spaniels, locked in battle and rolling down the lane past our front gate. But no, it was actually two young foxes. The growls and squeals persisted as they continued to roll out of sight, round the corner and eventually out of ear-shot. It was certainly a bizarre sight, and the like of which I'd not witnessed before, nor since. Spurred on by this reminder of the vulpine threat, I spent the day attending to the electric fencing around my chickens. The grass had started to sprout, and I knew there were several spots where it was producing the tell-tale 'tick', that indicated a place where it was 'earthing'. With the ground being so rough, there were a multitude of grassy tussocks which were not easy to remove. I had managed to get rid of the majority some weeks earlier, before I had set the fence up, but there were still plenty left that were near enough the fence to cause problems. And so I set about removing the turf from under the fence all the way around. This, I hoped, would free me up from constantly having to strim the grass on both sides of the 50m fence.

It was a hot and tiring job, but before too long I found myself surrounded by an attentive audience. The chickens, who had pretty much become hermits since their arrival, rarely leaving the comfort of their coop, could now hardly tear themselves away from what I was doing, and probably as a result spent their longest ever period outside to date.

As I worked beneath the gate I left it open, just for a moment.

"It's okay," I had shouted to Brian, "I can leave the gate open a bit and they won't come out. They're very territorial and Sandra said it took hers 6 months to venture out of their run when she first gave them the option."

However, Spence was a law unto himself (as we were to find out to our cost in the months ahead) and within a few minutes he had ducked past me and declared himself truly 'free-range'. Feeling very pleased with himself, he strutted back and forth, looking very important, whilst ensuring he kept at least a feather's width from recapture. The girls were less brave (or maybe sensible, in light of the fox incident that morning) and remained within the confines of the pen. Spence was on his own, and initially he seemed happy to show off to the girls from the other side of the fence.

The time came, however, when he hankered after the comforts of the coop and his harem, but it was at this point that he realised his error in failing to note the exact position of the gate, and a major panic set in. His 'cool dude' image was instantly shattered as he launched himself at the fence, ridiculously hoping to squeeze through one of the 10cm square holes in the netting. Humiliatingly for Spence, the only answer was for me to lift him over the fence, which did his 'street-cred' no good whatsoever. However, in an effort to regain some kind of authority, he fluffed his chest and neck feathers out and decided to eyeball a few of the girls. They were totally unimpressed as it happened, but it seemed to make *him* feel better.

If there was one thing we had a lot of on our smallholding, it was brambles; there were acres of them – or so it seemed. They encroached on the lower field in three massive patches, and on the top field they stretched almost the whole length of the field, in a wide swathe that dominated the top most edge of our land. Right from the beginning, before we'd moved in even, Brian had promised himself a spot up there; a place to sit and take in the magnificent views across the valley to Felinfawr Mountain. But first he needed to clear the brambles, and preferably before they started sprouting into growth again and spreading still further. He set to with the hand scythe on the top field, but this made no impact at all and he soon had to switch to snipping each individual stalk with the long-handled pruners. It was a gruelling, painstaking task, but it has to be said that great progress was made, and by the end of the first afternoon you could see a significant difference. The following day Brian resumed his work and all was going well, until he came across the most exquisite little nest, right in the middle of the patch he was clearing. He was alerted to it by the agitated calls of its architects, two long-tailed tits, who we watched take turns in sliding through a tiny hole in the side of the domed ball of moss and lichen and out again. Seeing their care and meticulous attention to detail, we hadn't the heart to destroy their efforts, and so work on that particular patch of brambles came to a halt for the foreseeable future. We would have to work around it until after the spring. Consulting our bird book, we were intrigued to read that the long-tailed tit makes its nest with cobwebs, and that the nest is designed to cleverly expand with the chicks as they grow! We looked forward to seeing this for ourselves over the coming months and marvelled at the ingenuity of nature.

March also saw Brian reach the landmark age of 60! It so happened that his birthday fell on a Wednesday, our regular volunteering day at the local Community Woodland, so I decided to make him a cake, appropriately themed in the shape of a tree stump, to take with us as a special surprise for Brian. Now, normally Brian would spend the days we were at home up in the veg patch or chopping up endless logs in the woodshed, but on the day before his birthday, when I needed him out of the kitchen and away from the house, he did neither. He sat and read his book, a monthly guide to jobs that need doing in the garden, and tried to decide whether he should plant some of the early potatoes he'd had chitting on the dining room window-sill. He also read the seed packets, to see if he could plant any of them in his greenhouse and he generally wandered in and out of the kitchen for hours. Therefore, I busied myself making apple crumble and strawberry jam (which was not a brilliant success) and preparing the vegetables for tea, and cleaning the bathrooms... in fact anything except what I really needed to do... whilst I waited for him to get outside, so I could start the cake. I even got the vacuum cleaner out and swept around him in the lounge - that usually did the trick - but no, not even that worked on this occasion. So eventually I just had to go for it and hope his poor observation skills would play to my advantage, which they did. He didn't notice that the mixture in the bowl was chocolate as he passed through the kitchen to fetch something, or that there were cake-tins in the sink when he came in to make a sandwich for lunch. However, I was careful to put the two chocolate cakes in the library to cool, as I thought that might be a bit of a giveaway and even Brian might question what I was doing. I eventually managed to put the cake together and decorate it with two shades of chocolate butter icing (a darker shade for the bark and a lighter one for the rings) by hiding it in the cupboard every time I heard the back door to the boot room open. It slowed the making process down considerably and it took me most of the day to achieve the finished result, but at last it was done. I then decided to put a snail on the side of the stump, made from fondant icing and painted with food colouring, which was a particularly fiddly job. It was at this point that Brian's visits to the kitchen became even more frequent, and I was starting to lose my patience. Strongly resisting the urge to strangle him, I locked myself in the bathroom so I could complete the snail in peace, and put it in the airing cupboard to dry.

The next morning, I got up early and made Brian a cup of tea in bed – well it *was* his birthday- and took the opportunity to transfer the snail from the airing cupboard to the cake, taking a couple of photos of the finished result whilst I could. All that remained to be done was to get the cake into the car without

Brian seeing, which I did when he took Storm for his morning walk up the lane.

When I produced the cake during our lunchtime break, sitting around the campfire in the middle of the wood, with the rest of the gang, it all proved worthwhile. He was totally taken aback and seemed rather chuffed by the whole thing. Rob, our lead warden, then decided to abandon the work schedule in preference for a besom-making competition, as it was Brian's birthday, and showed us what we needed to do. We worked in pairs or small groups to produce some very fine brooms that any self-respecting witch would have been proud of; it was great fun, with plenty of friendly banter thrown back and forth. We could have brought our fine broom home with us, but Brian, being a big softee at heart, decided to donate it to one of the younger lads who'd struggled to make his broom. It was certainly an alternative way to spend your 60th birthday, but certainly one to remember.

~

With the duck eggs due to hatch in a couple of days, Brian was already contemplating the next project – geese. This was definitely Brian's project, as geese were not top of my loves, having been chased on a regular basis by a group of geese that used to lay in wait for me on my way to primary school. As these were to be meat birds, Brian was keen to go for one of the larger breeds (joy!) and plumped for the Toulouse. I must admit they appeared to be good looking birds, and on further investigation they were apparently 'a docile breed ideal for the novice', which all bode well for a reasonably harmonious co-existence.

After much searching and several enquiries via email, I tracked down some reasonably priced Toulouse hatching-eggs at £1.50 each. We probably only needed four in order to get two or maybe three geese, but with the new fully automated incubator, we had no idea as to its efficiency. However, we did have our ducks due to hatch in a couple of days, so we'd soon know.

The signs were all good. Having finished turning the eggs on the 26th day of incubation, we awoke the next morning to one or two of the eggs rocking, as the ducklings started the long task of tapping their way out of their shells. I increased the humidity to 80%, to ensure the membranes didn't dry out and become too tough, hindering the hatching process.

We tried to contain our excitement at the imminent arrival of our first ducklings at Nantcoed and did our best to keep ourselves occupied. I was busy painting our bedroom (not very successfully as it happens, as the colour turned out to be far too dark, and the whole room would need to be repainted the following day with a lighter tone) and Brian was planting his peas, arranging his pea sticks and other important things like that. But throughout the day we were both drawn to the dining room for sneaky peeks through the incubator window and updates on progress.

By four o'clock we noticed the first egg had 'pipped'. Later, at bedtime, several were rocking and four or five were 'pipped'. You could also hear the ducklings calling from inside their eggs, encouraging each other. You can't help but be amazed at the whole process, however many times you've seen it before.

By the next morning one duckling had managed to push its tiny pink beak out through the shell and it looked like this one would be first to hatch, but progress was slow. I struggled to get the humidity up to 80% and I was worried the membranes of those that had pipped would start to dry out, making it really difficult for the ducklings to get out, so I laid a warm, wet cloth over the eggs, mimicking the wet feathers of the mother duck. This worked a treat and soon we had several exhausted, yellow babies draped across the incubator floor. Not, however, the one that had been first to push its beak through the shell; this bird seemed to be making no progress whatsoever. By the evening we had six hatched and two close to hatching, not counting the one that appeared stuck. I waited up late for these two to hatch and dry off a bit, not wanting to leave them in the incubator all night. Once each duckling was reasonably dry and fluffed up, I transferred them to a brooder box that I had set up in the dining room. It was just a large plastic storage box with a lid, a small pot of water, sawdust and an 'electric hen' (which we'd recently bought, as it was a tenth of the cost of running the heat lamp). This consisted of a metal rectangular heat pad on four

37

adjustable legs, that enabled you to raise the heat pad as the birds grew in size. By the time we went to bed the duckling that was stuck had still not made any progress and I decided the time had come to intervene – this is very frowned upon in some circles, but as I was not intending to breed from these ducks, and I wanted the best outcome possible, I didn't hesitate. As anyone who has hatched eggs will know, you can't just cut a duckling out of its shell, because breaking the membrane would cause it to bleed to death. You have to work slowly and carefully. I had done this many times before when we'd hatched call-ducks.

Finally, I managed to ease the duckling out and leave it in the incubator to fluff up. However, it soon became evident that all was not well and the poor thing could not seem to straighten its neck, and one of its legs appeared completely useless. This could explain why it had had so much trouble hatching; maybe it would have been kinder to have left it in its egg. We would probably have to euthanase it in the morning, but I left it in the warmth of the incubator, along with the one other egg still to hatch.

The next morning the dog was barking at 5am, so I got up to see what he was barking at and to check on progress in the incubator. The poorly duckling was lying on its side, looking no better, and the unhatched egg was still unhatched. I decided the last egg would need some help, as it had got nowhere. The egg was very dry and easy to open at one end. I wondered if I was doing the right thing; maybe this duckling would be disabled too. However, when this one emerged it was perfectly fine, just exhausted, and I was glad I had helped it out. I then went back to bed, leaving the two ducklings in the incubator.

When I got up just after 7am though, the disabled duckling had made a miraculous recovery and could now straighten its neck and was trying to use its poorly leg. I couldn't believe the change! Both ducklings were transferred to the brooder and within a few hours it was really difficult to spot the one that had come so close to being put out of its misery. I was so glad that I had given it time to recover overnight. So, we now had ten gorgeous fluffy yellow ducklings – not a bad success rate from twelve eggs.

But these sweet looking babies, were not as cute as they'd like you to believe. No, they are the messiest critters I know! At one day old we moved the ducklings out to a run in the garage that I had prepared, with lovely clean newspaper topped with fresh sawdust, a water drinker and a small feeder of chick crumbs. I also transferred their 'electric hen' so that they would be warm and cosy.

However, just half an hour later, they had trashed the whole lot! They were in the water, literally, and dashing to and fro scattering chick crumbs and water in every direction! And it was only going to get worse as they grew.

A typical duckling day appeared to consist of sleeping in a heap (either under the 'electric hen', or on top - for those that preferred the luxury of under-floor heating) followed by short frantic bursts of activity, which basically involved spreading water and excrement to every corner of the run and pecking at anything that remotely resembled food, including the mucky splashes on the wooden sides of the enclosure, and even the eyes of their siblings. Then everyone would suddenly collapse, exhausted by their exertions, with beaks resting on neighbours' backs and feet extending backwards, as if enjoying the sheer pleasure of being able to stretch at full length after their weeks of confinement in a tight shell. The tranquillity of sleeping ducklings however, was all too brief, and shortly, with batteries recharged, the next bout of vandalism ensued. As a result, the water drinker needed constant replenishment, the run was a sodden mess within seconds of me cleaning it and there was the emergence of a somewhat permanent lake in the centre of the garage floor. I was already looking forward to the time we could move them outside, to their beautiful purpose-built run.

Even by day 2, you could see a marked increase in the ducklings' size. At night I put the heat lamp on to give them some extra warmth, gradually raising it every couple of days, so the ducklings got used to a lower ambient temperature. Of course they still had the 'electric hen' to snuggle under too.

~

Since our move to Wales, we had been blessed with more than our fair share of rain; in fact it had rained for what seemed like weeks, and we were beginning to wonder if moving to the mountains of Wales had been such a good idea after all, especially as Brian hated the rain and loved to feel the sunshine on his back. But March turned out to be unbelievably dry, and towards the end of the month we saw the most glorious sunny mornings and warm, even hot, days. There was lots of talk on the news about hosepipe bans in East Anglia and the Midlands, and even our little stream was much diminished, despite the huge volume of water it had seen over the winter. Unbelievably, Brian was caught saying, 'What we could do with is some rain!' as he studied the raised beds in his veg plot.

It was on one of these wonderfully sunny mornings, as we were enjoying a cup of tea in bed, prior to facing the chores of the day, that we heard Spence's first attempts at crowing. His performance still needed some fine tuning and was more than a little rough at the edges, but the opening line of 'Cock-a' was perfect. The end however, disintegrated into a sort of mumble, as if he'd forgotten the words. 'Cock-a-roo-er-oo,' came his muffled crow from the still closed-up chicken coop. 'Cock-a-roo-er-oo,' he gave with enthusiastic gusto. These first earnest efforts had us rolling about in stitches, and we flung open the bedroom window wide, so we could fully appreciate the entertainment on offer – a good chuckle certainly gets the day off to a great start!

Despite Spence's vocal difficulties, he certainly seemed to have won the respect of the girls, and all was contentment in the chicken pen. The unusually warm weather brought on a frenzy of dust baths under the coop, as well as in a number of other spots around the run which had become dotted with several ankle-turning craters, and the whole gang spent much more time outside enjoying the sunshine. The girls followed Spence wherever he went, swooning with renewed admiration. Yes, he had definitely got their attention.

Over the following days and weeks Spence tried a variety of early morning calls in an effort to get it *just right*. We had 'Cock-a-roo-al' and 'Cock-a-roo-er-er' and something that sounded more like an impression of Tarzan swinging through the jungle than a cockerel. The entertainment was endless, as was Spence's improvisation and artistic interpretation.

Meanwhile the girls were also providing us with their own brand of entertainment. I loved to watch the chickens as they mooched, muttering contentment and stepping daintily amongst the tussocks of grass, as if picking their way in classy high heels. It is all an act of course; their true colours instantly revealed should one of them discover something out of the ordinary - a piece of apple or a particularly tasty slug perhaps - when all signs of 'dainty' are but a mirage, as five overweight fish-wives in 'January Sales mode' thunder across the pen with huge, ungainly strides and legs flung with reckless abandon to left and right. With heads down and necks at full stretch they run 'hell for leather' to claim the morsel as their own, before anyone else can get their beak on it, the veil of elegance extinguished in a flash.

~

The dry weather at last gave us the chance to investigate the problems we'd been having with our septic tank system since we'd moved in. There appeared to be three tanks which eventually drained into the field, or not in this case. With the land falling away from the house at a decent gradient, gravity should have simply taken the liquids through the soil, which would then filter them. The previous owner had also planted a good number of bulrushes in an effort to create a reed bed. Unfortunately bulrushes are not the reeds you need for a proper, efficient reed bed and we had not been able to get our hands on the right type, as yet. With Brian's fishery background, and with one of our fisheries actually running a reed bed sewage filtration system, he luckily knew what he was doing, which is always a good start! The ground, up to now, had been far too wet to contemplate this job, and there was a good deal of puddling of effluent which was both unsightly and smelly. Proper channels needed to be dug, a layer of stones created and pipes with holes laid on top. This would ensure the fluids were quickly dispersed so that the field could filter them properly. As it was, the heavy clay soil was completely clogging the system, and nothing seemed to be draining anywhere. It was a hot and

41

smelly job, but we were determined to take advantage of the long dry spell – we didn't know when we might get another chance.

Now, there are '*my* jobs' and there are '*his* jobs', but very few '*our* jobs' (as I had wisely been advised by a fellow smallholder, soon after we'd moved - and she was indeed right). It is, as it turns out, always best to establish who is in charge from the beginning, if you are to avoid a barrage of irritable comments and a less than harmonious atmosphere. Unfortunately, in error, I supposed that this job was a *joint* effort (what was I thinking?) and kindly offered my opinion as to the direction of flow and some possible solutions. These comments however, were not received as they had been intended, and I was firmly told by Brian, that he'd been *doing drainage* for some years and should know what he was doing by now. Of course ladies, we know that this is actually a 'no-win' situation, because if you try to be helpful you get the response I received, but if you don't offer your opinion and it all goes 'belly-up', you are invariably asked why you didn't give your opinion at the time, instead of watching him flounder.

Anyway, as it turned out, Brian *did* know what he was doing and the only purpose of me attending this little 'get-together' by the cess-pit was to provide a 'go-for' service; which was actually fine by me, because I'm really good at fetching things, and I really didn't feel that being knee deep in a sewage soakaway was really my thing. S**t (human or bull) I felt, was definitely Brian's forté!

5. Highs and lows

April began with talk of frost, rain and snow - what perfect timing, as ever, with a week of visitors ahead of us!

We already had our youngest home from uni for a few days, before he headed back to Herefordshire to see his friends and earn some money with a 'holiday job' at a petrol station. Then we had my parents coming to see our new home for the first time and stay overnight; being in their eighties, they had sensibly waited until 'the warmer weather', which obviously didn't pan out quite as they'd expected. And then, the day after my parents' departure, we had our eldest and his girlfriend coming for the Easter weekend, and hopefully to build us a 'Whizbang Chicken Plucker'. A little warm sunshine would have really gone down a treat, but typically, with a Bank Holiday on the horizon, it was not to be and we had the two coldest and wettest days we'd had for weeks on the exact same two days that my parents came to stay; in fact they ended up returning home at lunchtime on the second day, worried about the prospect of snow and the possibility of getting stranded! They'd have been welcome to stop longer, and return home the next day when the weather was supposed to see some improvement, but Brian hurt his back badly that morning whilst walking the dog; Storm had lunged at one of the local farmer's dogs as it ran behind its owner's Landrover, jerking the lead and twisting Brian's back suddenly. As a result, Mum and Dad decided they'd be best out of the way.

We had only had a small flurry of snow in the morning, but the wind was bitterly cold. However, Mum and Dad ended up travelling through two or three inches of snow, not just over the Welsh mountains, but all the way home to Shropshire; a somewhat nightmare journey for them, which probably only served to confirm any worries they had had about us living in an inaccessible place, miles away from them.

It was lovely to see them, but gutting that it had been so wet and cold that Dad had hardly been able to venture further than the kitchen door, and so didn't really get a chance to fully explore our new home. Mum, valiant as always, had donned her cagoule and wellies, and with brolly aloft forged out into the elements for a guided tour, and to help me feed the chickens. Hopefully in the short time they were with us, they had gained *some* appreciation of what we were trying to achieve on our Welsh smallholding. And hopefully next time they visited the weather would be a lot more amenable.

~

At just two weeks of age our ducklings were getting quite big - you could almost *see* them growing! They were still enjoying playing in the drinker and managing to reduce everything to 'mush' in a very short space of time, so when the weather improved (the day *after* Mum and Dad had returned home in the snow) and the sun brought us a lovely warm day, I put the ducklings outside in their run. As they were still covered in down and not yet waterproof, I did not connect the water to their 'stream' for fear of them becoming chilled, but they still had their beloved drinker. They relished it out there and, surprise surprise, made a bee-line for the two small (and very muddy) puddles in the bottom of the empty 'stream'. Within milliseconds of their release, their beaks and yellow, downy chests were black, but they were so pleased with themselves you couldn't help but smile! It was good to see them with the sun on their backs and stretching their stubby little wings. With the recent frosty nights of course, I had had to use the heat lamp more than I'd wanted to, and until the ducklings had their proper feathers they couldn't stay outside permanently, but when the weather allowed they were treated to time in the run and the garage was given some welcome respite.

It was as I was watching the ducklings one day, that I heard a minor commotion over in the chicken pen. On closer investigation I discovered Maisie wandering through the long grass on the *wrong* side of the electric fence. She appeared to have flapped her wings rather harder than was needed and overshot the fence! The chickens often flapped their wings as an aid to increase velocity when dashing across the pen for whatever reason they felt speed was of the essence, and sometimes, no doubt aided by the extra lift that being on a hillside afforded them, they would surprise themselves by launching into the air briefly, but there was probably no-one more surprised than Maisie to now find herself on the outside of the fence looking in. I lifted her back over the fence and hoped that this was just a one-off miscalculation.

Jack and Ellie's arrival signalled the start of the big Whizbanger building project. Jack had done his homework and we had ordered all the parts we needed, but he only had three days to get it built, before he had to return to work. The Whizbanger would consist of a blue plastic barrel cut in half and fitted with rubber 'fingers', ingeniously connected to a system of pulleys and an old washing machine motor that would propel the barrel at varying speeds in a circular motion. When combined with a hosepipe it should be possible to pluck a bird in less than a minute! He set himself up in the garage, right next to the ducklings (which was a tad insensitive when you think about it, as the ducks would be the first to experience the Whizbanger in action).

By the end of the weekend the plucker was complete and tested, as best you can without a bird to put in it; we improvised with a rolled up bath towel tied with string and wetted to achieve something like the correct weight. All we needed now was the real thing – but that would be another six weeks away yet.

~

In the short time since we'd arrived in Felinfawr, we had made a good many friends. There was Dewi, who owned the sheep in the fields surrounding us, and his son Aled, who would arrive regularly on his quad bike to see to the sheep and lambs. We always knew when Aled was around, as his presence was announced loudly by a chorus of excited bleating issuing from every field, in the hope that his visit was one of those when he brought bags of feed with him; sheep are obviously not as dim as some imagine. We had got to know Dewi quite well, from our attendance at the short mat bowls evenings at the village hall. He was a friendly welsh farmer with a twinkle of mischief in his eye. He had tried hard to persuade me to join the jive classes at the village hall, and his enthusiasm for the dance appeared quite incongruous with the figure that stood before us.

It was Dewi that we were grateful to when it came to the safety of our chickens, though not because he kept the fox numbers at bay. Dewi kept chickens himself, but rarely shut them away at night, so the fox often got a free meal. As he lived at the far end of the wood from us, we had come to the conclusion that as long as Dewi had chickens, ours would be relatively safe, as the fox would take the easy pickings at his place, rather than tackle our electric poultry fence (or so the theory went). Consequently, we would often ask Dewi how many chickens he had left, and only worry when the answer was 'just two now'. However, our hopes would lift again when he added, 'But I'm going to pick some more up next week'.

Of course we had seen evidence of foxes in our garden, and Brian had spotted the odd fox on more than one occasion whilst taking the dog out in the morning, and so we were always keen to find someone who would shoot them. Dewi, it appeared, had a shotgun, and he certainly had a motive, but after hearing about his past attempts at marksmanship, our hopes of him being the answer to our problems were sorely shattered. He told us how he had once lain in wait in the field, with the wind favourably towards him and so disguising his scent, when a fox came straight towards him. When it was within just a few metres of him he had 'let it have both barrels'. However, the shot was so off target, despite the close proximity of hunter and hunted, that the fox had merely paused, and looked up quizzically, sensing that something may have just passed over its head, before it continued on its way.

Of course it was not just the chickens we needed to worry about. There is nothing a fox likes better than a tasty duck. At three weeks of age our ducklings had outgrown the area we'd given them in the garage, and as it was still not warm enough to put them outside permanently, I had to work on expanding the run to allow them a much bigger space. Their drinker was now needing to be filled several times a day, so I decided to get them a much bigger one; they now had a massive ten litres to spread about, instead of just one litre, and of course the result was an even larger indoor lake. It was about now that we started praying seriously for some warmer weather and for the ducklings' feathers to grow! Hopefully it wouldn't be too long.

Meanwhile, back in the incubator we now had 6 huge goose eggs, which were due to hatch in 2 - 3 weeks; as they can take anything between 28 and 35 days we couldn't be absolutely certain when to expect the new arrivals. It seemed likely however, that there would be little respite for the garage floor between ducklings and goslings. The quality of our goose eggs was in question though, as when 'candled' the results had been dubious to say the least. We had paid £1.50 per egg and the farm we had collected them from was a rather haphazard affair it seemed. To start with the farmer's wife was unsure as to whether the goslings would be pure Toulouse or Toulouse x Embden, as the Embden had 'got in with' the Toulouse. As far as we could see, all the birds appeared to roam where they liked and they *all* 'got in with' each other. Then when we had handed over the money, we were presented with the dirtiest looking eggs we'd ever seen.

Before setting the eggs in the incubator, I had read that it was a good idea to clean them with warm water; it should be warmer than the egg to prevent bacteria travelling through the porous shell and infecting the potential embryo. I had also read that goose eggs differ from those of ducks and chickens, in that you shouldn't set them point down in the incubator, but on their side, and that you should only turn them pointed end to pointed end, 180 degrees, rather than roll them sideways. All this we did, but when we candled them at 10 days expecting to see a web of blood vessels, we just saw a dark shadow which was probably the yolk, so the fertility of these eggs remained in question.

However, when I candled them again at 14 days I was heartened to see that four of the eggs had signs of a few blood vessels and the dark area seemed to be bigger. Strangely, each of the four potentially fertile eggs had blood vessels that formed a cross like a kiss. The duck eggs had had a web of much smaller vessels, but having not incubated goose eggs before, I had no idea if this was normal - only time would tell. Another worry was the noise that our 'all singing, all dancing' incubator was making. The fan appeared to be struggling, and at times was making quite a noise and vibrating violently. Vibration is not good when incubating eggs and in the end I switched it off and back on again (the well documented solution for most technical problems) which seemed to do the trick, for a while anyway. I just hoped it would hold out for another two or three weeks.

The 14th April was a long awaited day - we had the first egg from our chickens! I was in the garage, building a stall to put out by the front gate, from which to sell our excess produce (another of my little projects) and Brian appeared with a cup of tea for me around midday. I decided to take my drink up to the chalet, and sit under the canopy in order to dodge the intermittent showers that had made a nuisance of themselves all that morning. I sat looking at the view across the valley, and watching the chickens on the slope below me picking their way across the tussocks in their pen. A minor disturbance from within the coop soon interrupted this tranquil scene, and drew the attention of both human and chicken. The panic call, generally reserved for warning of lowing flying crows or buzzards, froze all movement just for a fraction of a second. I swiftly scanned the pen and realised that one chicken was missing. It was either Meg or Pippy, it was hard to tell from a distance, who emerged a tad flustered, fluffing her feathers out as if having just escaped a close shave. It warranted further investigation, so putting my mug down I made my way over to the pen, where to my delight I discovered the most perfect little egg sitting in the nest box! Okay, it *was* little, but it was perfectly formed and even laid in the right place -pretty impressive. I had read that to start with chickens can get caught short and lay their first few eggs just about anywhere. I obviously had a much more intelligent strain.

I couldn't wait to show Brian; perhaps now he would stop casting aspersions on my chickens' ability to do their bit towards our self-sufficiency. We decided we would have the egg boiled (with soldiers of course) and share it between us. I boiled it for just 3mins and presented it in an egg cup (which I must admit swamped the egg somewhat) and served it on a small plate with soldiers, flanked by two teaspoons. It was the tastiest egg I think I have ever tasted (not that I'm biased of course). The next question was, would there be eggs tomorrow, and if so how many?

The next morning, I went out to the chicken coop with expectant anticipation, but my hopes were sadly dashed. We had no eggs at all that day. But the following morning when I went to let the chickens out and clean the coop, there was another little egg in the nest box. The following day straining noises issued from the coop, and about a quarter of an hour later I noticed that all five chickens were out with Spence, so I hotfooted it up to the pen to see if an egg had been produced. Feeling positive, I took a scoop of mixed corn with me as a reward. I scattered the corn and then peered into the nest box, but there was no egg. Around teatime I popped up again, and this time I was greeted with not one, but three eggs; one in the nest box - good girl - and two by the drinker, obviously the result of being caught short. These two eggs were very small. The egg in the nest box was a little bigger than previous ones. It was all very exciting!

The excitement was short-lived however, as Brian hurt his back again. He was just bending over to look at his potatoes (as you do) to check if they were growing yet, and he felt it go. Brian had suffered with his back on and off for years, but this time it was more serious. Within minutes he could not move. Luckily he'd made it back to the house, but despite hot water bottles and massages, he could not move from the sofa. I have never seen him in so much pain. He would never normally even consider taking painkillers, but this time he was begging for them, and when his back went into spasm his eyes reflected the agony he was enduring, as they widened and stared straight ahead. In the past he had flatly refused to go for treatment, but this time, thank goodness, it was different. A quick call to Karina, one of our new friends who lived on the mountain, supplied us with the name and telephone number of Dee. I was reassured by Karina that Dee worked in a very 'gentle' way. She was apparently a trained physiotherapist, but also used a holistic approach. I carefully omitted to tell Brian about the holistic bit, as I thought that might be a step too far for my very conventional husband. I rang Dee, who was busy putting up a new polytunnel. Being on top of the mountain they apparently had a lot of trouble with plants being, literally, blown out of the ground! Dee said she would be over to see us in a couple of hours.

When she arrived she managed to slowly coax Brian off the sofa and onto her portable couch, where she massaged his back and looked for the root of his problem. I'm pleased to say Brian felt a lot more comfortable afterwards and I hoped he was convinced enough to give it another go in a couple of days, as she had suggested, when things weren't so uptight and sore.

Amazingly, he did call her the next day and made a further appointment for later in the week. Unfortunately, we had been due to visit Brian's Mum, and meet up with our youngest son over in Ledbury, the day after Brian hurt his back, but there was no way that Brian would make it, and I couldn't go on my own and leave him all day to fend for himself, so we had to postpone the visit. However, he hoped to be well enough by the end of the week, to make the two and a half hour journey, but I seriously had my doubts.

With Brian out of action, it was left to me to keep the place running as best I could, as well as caring for my husband's every need. It was exhausting! I found I was having to get up at 7am (as opposed to the 9am I generally rolled out of bed these days) in order to get all the animals fed and cleaned out before breakfast. There was starter-wood to chop and the fire to lay, logs to move from the various spots outside that Brian had them drying, the greenhouse to open and close, seeds to water, the newspaper to fetch from the post-office in the village, hot water bottles to fill, cups of tea to make, meals to prepare, eggs to collect and escaped chickens to return safely to the pen. Why, I don't know, but Flossie, one of our Buff Sussex seemed to be making a regular habit of launching herself over the three-foot high electric fence. Having not actually seen her do it, it was difficult to appreciate whether this was a recurring accident or a concerted effort to find pastures new. This said, it did seem a dippy idea, which Flossie (the blondest of our girls I'm sorry to admit) seemed unable to grasp; after all, both the food and her friends were on the inside of the fence, and as soon as she had catapulted herself over she found herself intent on trying to get back, as Spence paced back and forth in some distress on the inside. The worry was of course that she might perform this trick when we were not around and offer herself as a tasty snack for a passing fox.

When all the animals were fed and watered, fresh, dry bedding replenished (briefly in the case of the ducklings) and Brian settled with a new hot water bottle and a cup of tea in front of the TV, I was able to work on my latest project in the garage - the building of the stall, from which I hoped to sell surplus fruit and veg from the garden, herb plants and eggs from our chickens (once they were a decent size). I worked to the accompaniment of contented grunts coming from the ducks as they cocked a quizzical eye in my direction. The framework was made from lengths of 2"x2" and the 'counter' and roof from some plywood we had left over from building the chicken coop. The back wall I put together from pallet wood, scavenged from the local tip. I bought two wheelbarrow wheels from the ironmongers shop in town, and mounted these to the legs at one end, and covered the roof with some red checked oil-cloth discovered in the same shop. There were also two handles, so you could easily wheel the whole thing back and forth to the gate, and I cannibalised a lockable metal money box, cutting a slot in the top, and screwed it to the back wall of the stall for people to post their payments into. I was rather pleased with how it was looking and all that remained was for me to paint it a light, fern green. I had also painted some odd lengths of plywood with blackboard paint and cut some beading to form a border. These, I anticipated putting on the roadside, so I could advertise to passers-by what I had for sale on the stall. Being on a school run, I hoped we would have quite a few customers and raise at least enough to cover the cost of feed for our chickens. Others in the village had told me how they managed to sell their eggs without any difficulty, some on very quiet lanes where you'd think nobody passed all day. It was certainly worth a go. Now we just needed some proper sized eggs to sell.

But when I went down to let the chickens out the next morning, I was greeted with two broken eggs right by the door. On closer investigation I could see that the shells of both were soft. This was a blow, and after clearing up the mess and completing my long list of jobs, I investigated further on the internet as to the possible reasons for getting soft shells. It appeared there were three possible causes; the first I discounted, as it referred to disease and indicated that the birds would look unwell, which my birds definitely didn't, rather they were blooming with health; the second possible cause was a shock provoked by the chickens being caught in a sudden heavy shower, which seemed a possibility; the third however, I felt was the one that made most sense - the fact that these might be the first eggs that two of the chickens had laid, and that their bodies hadn't quite got into the swing of it all yet. This could mean that all our chickens had now started laying - which was great news!

The following morning I discovered two more broken eggs near the door, though this time the shells were hard. Well, this was a slight improvement, but the worry was that the chickens would get a liking for the taste of eggs and get into the habit of eating their own eggs. We appeared to have two chickens who had not worked out what the nest boxes were for yet, so I decided to give them a bit of a hint by placing a golf ball in one of the nest boxes, amongst the wood shavings. When I returned at lunchtime, I was pleased to see two beautiful eggs laid in the nest box with the golf ball! There were none in the box without the golf ball, despite this having been the preferred box on previous occasions; pretty convincing evidence I think, for the success of golf balls.

A few days later, Brian's back was feeling a lot better and we were able to make our trip to Ledbury at long last. At the unearthly hour of 6am, when it was still not properly light, the chickens stared in bleary-eyed disbelief as I hassled them off their perches and out into the rain. Some flatly refused to move, and stubbornly stood just where I was trying to clean, feigning complete ignorance of my urgency to get the job done. However, despite the truculence of the chickens and the antics of the ducklings, we managed to be on the road by 8am and in Ledbury by 10.30am.

After a long day of catching up with friends and relatives, and another two and a half hour journey home, we returned weary and ready to put our feet up. However, there were the usual duties to be performed before we could contemplate a rest. With the light fading fast I approached the chicken pen, to find there was one chicken on the wrong side of the electric fence yet again - this was becoming a habit - but for once it wasn't Flossie, but Pippi. After several fruitless dives and lunges, much to the amusement of my beloved husband, I eventually managed to grab the miscreant as she attempted to squeeze through one of the small rectangles in the electric netting, displaying a woefully disillusioned appreciation of her own body image.

With the ducklings fed and watered, the dog let out to relieve himself, the fire lit and the cat let in to stretch herself out in front of it, we could finally put our feet up; it had been a long day.

6.Ducks!

The ducklings were gradually becoming whiter as they started to get their proper feathers through, well that is if you caught them after a preening session early in the day, before they had reduced their run in the garage to a quagmire of slurry. Our lot were also very agile for ducks; one morning, whilst I was busy scooping up the soggy mess they had created overnight, I swung around to find one large duckling actually sat on top of the shavings in my bucket, looking very pleased with himself. Sometimes it was hard not to get attached to these comical birds and I had to harden my resolve if I was to see the duck project through to the end.

The smallholding was well under way and we felt pleased to have achieved so much in what was quite a short space of time. We had chickens and ducklings, and soon would be welcoming our first geese into the world. With everything going so well, it was inevitable I suppose, that some catastrophe was just around the corner.

Our goose eggs had less than a week to go before they were due to hatch, and having tended to their every need for the past 26 days, the incubator, which had been threatening for days to break down, did just that. The fan started making the most alarming noise, making the whole unit vibrate. I switched it off and back on again, as I had done several times that week, so that the motor would revert to its normal function. This time however, it didn't. Brian had just made a hot water bottle to ease his still uncomfortable back, so I requisitioned it and grabbed a couple of hand towels, to keep the eggs warm whilst I tinkered with the fan – not that I had a clue what I was doing of course! I hoped that perhaps something had become lodged in the fan, or maybe it had become loose, but alas there was no such simple solution. It was definitely dead. This of course left us with the tricky problem of keeping the eggs not just warm, but at the correct temperature of 37.5°C.

I rigged up the heat lamp over the curtain rail in the dining room, and pushed the dining table towards the window so that I could put the bottom of the incubator, complete with eggs, under the lamp. There then followed three hours of tweaking with the height of the lamp and attempting to read the ridiculously minuscule scale on the thermometer, in an effort to achieve the optimum temperature. Of course the humidity would be very poor, at a time when it really mattered, but there was nothing I could do about that. I would ring the supplier first thing in the morning to discuss a replacement. In the meantime, I scoured the internet for some idea of possible replacements, should it come to that. A back up incubator would be a good idea, I surmised, but could we afford the luxury? I hoped I would have time to sort it all out first thing, as I had a busy and stressful day planned as it was.

Firstly, it was my turn to help with the WI refreshments in the evening and I had ham sandwiches, cocktail sausages and crisps to provide, which would involve a trip to town for ingredients, as well as preparation time. Joining the WI was one of the first things I had done when we arrived in Felinfawr. It had only taken one visit to realise that Felinfawr WI were not like any other; they were a quirky lot (in the nicest possible way) and so welcoming...I just knew I'd fit in fine and there would be a lot of fun along the way. Not the staid old flower-arranging and slides of 'British jugs since 1850' for this lot! No. Low wire walking and belly dancing were more their game. I never realised WI could be so much fun! Even reading the minutes from the last meeting became a highlight when Carol was scribing. Her dry humour and fantastical embellishments added a uniquely entertaining element to the mildly recognisable occurrences of our previous meeting. If you had missed the last meeting, for whatever reason, you could be left mildly bewildered as to what had apparently occurred in your absence, not to mention 'gutted' that you'd missed such high jinks, which only sufficed to encourage a good attendance at subsequent get-togethers.

I had also (rashly perhaps) offered my services to a fellow WI refreshment maker, who had forgotten when she had volunteered, that she had a quick turnaround to achieve for her holiday barn, and who was going to struggle to attend the evening. As she was the only one out of the two of us who knew what she was doing (this being my first time of doing the refreshments) I was keen that she was able to stay and see us through it. Anyway, I offered to help her prepare the barn for the next guests.

The following morning I was up early, in order to get the dog, cat, chickens and ducks sorted before 9am, so that I could fully concentrate on sorting out the incubator problem, prior to running some errands and helping out at the holiday-let. There was good news and bad news when I called the supplier of our incubator; yes they would fix the fan for us under the 12 month warranty, even though we had bought it 13 months ago, but they could not help with the loan of an incubator in the meantime. This meant we had to put Plan B into action.

Plan B was unfortunately the more expensive option, of purchasing another incubator which would become a backup in the event of any future breakdowns, should we be faced with a similar dilemma in the future. I eventually managed to track down a company that could supply us with an incubator by the following morning, guaranteed, and placed the order without delay. Of course we didn't know whether the embryos had actually survived the night under the 'Heath Robinson' lamp arrangement on the dining table, or indeed whether they could possibly withstand yet another 24 hours, but we figured we had to give them every chance, and a back up incubator was probably sensible whatever the outcome of this particular clutch of eggs.

I turned the eggs a few times during the day, ensuring that both sides were getting heated, and I splashed them with warm water intermittently throughout the day too.

Before collapsing into bed that night, I candled the eggs in the hope of seeing some movement, though it seemed as if we were grasping at woefully fragile straws. Incredibly though, as the strong light penetrated the shells of three eggs, silhouettes clearly jumped and twitched with life, and our hopes soared. We may just have got away with it after all!

By half past ten the following morning, the new incubator had arrived and I hurriedly set it up and transferred the eggs. I increased the humidity to 60% in the hope of compensating for the dry atmosphere the eggs had endured over the previous forty hours. There was no more I could do, but hope that luck was on our side.

I went about the daily chores that morning with just a little more optimism. Outside, I set about reclaiming the garage, having carried the ducks, two by two (one under each arm) down to their purpose built, luxury pen, complete with lush reseeded grass and fresh running water. The weather was wet and miserable, but the ducks appeared to have enough feathers now to cope with the elements, and keeping them in the garage was really becoming untenable. It had become such a wet and smelly space, despite replacing their sawdust twice daily. They would be far better outside, and indeed would surely love it. I just knew I could no longer continue the daily struggle to protect the other contents of the garage from imminent flood or gaseous suffocation any longer.

It took me four hours to get the garage clean, disinfected and somewhere near 'normal' again, by which time I was ready for a well deserved lunch. However, before retiring to the kitchen, I thought I'd better just check that the ducks were okay in their lovely new home.

What met my eyes was more than shocking (though I could hardly be a surprised). Where there had been lush green grass, there was now nothing but liquid mud! The 'stream' outlet was totally blocked with debris and bubbling over the sides. The carefully positioned stones that had created a platform for ease of exit from the water, were now scattered far and wide and every corner of the pen was totally trashed!

The vandals stopped mid-action and stood stock still, their gaze meeting mine. As reality dawned, guilt swept across each beady eye. They shuffled uncomfortably, trying to convey an air of complete innocence, futile in view of the overwhelming weight of evidence against them, as muddy drips hovered from the stubby ends of little outstretched wings and dark brown aprons obliterated any semblance of white plumage or purity.

I could have wept.

I stood for some time in the rain, rivulets dribbling down my face, surveying the state of the pen and the ducks, and considering my next move. One thing was for sure, after four long hours of cleaning up the garage, they were *not* returning there.

I decided to consider my options over lunch, but there was no 'light bulb moment', and as the forecast was for a let up in the rain by evening, followed by a mainly dry day, I decided to leave them where they were. Overnight they would be in their house, which was lovely and clean and dry, as none of the ducks had had the courage to venture in there as yet (probably because they were having such a good time outside!) Hopefully the breeze would help to dry the ground a little. In a vain effort to improve the situation, after the ducks were safely tucked up in their house for the night, I skimmed the worst of the mud off the top of the grass, with a broom and a spade.

The weather had been so wet over the previous few days, that even the chickens were struggling with puddles and muddy patches in their run. Remarkably though, the chickens seemed undaunted by the wet, and, unless actually egg laying, continued to spend most of their day outside; that is, except for when the rain fell like stair rods, at which juncture an undignified dash ensued, necks outstretched and legs akimbo to left and right, as each raced to 'bagsy' a coveted space under the coop until the squall had passed. Space under the coop was at a premium, since the deep hollows excavated for communal dust-bathing on drier days were now transformed into plunge pools by the persistent rain, leaving very little standing room.

The chickens were a constant source of amusement to us and we spent endless hours, cup of tea in hand, watching their antics from two director-style seats tucked under the canopy of the little wooden chalet. Spence had grown into a magnificent and proud cockerel, and although he still hadn't quite got the words right when he crowed, he was a virile young male, always on the look-out for an opportunity to prove his manliness. Unfortunately, like many a teenager, he had not yet perfected the art of good love-making and lacked any subtlety in his approach. He would emerge from the coop in the morning as soon as I opened the door, ready to jump on the first living thing he could pin down. The girls on the other hand, just wanted to stretch their wings, have a drink and wake up slowly; it was too early for anything else as far as they were concerned. And so a morning ritual developed, whereby Spence, ready for action, would eagerly await the emergence of the first girl from the coop. There was a general reluctance by the girls to be 'the one', but either someone would emerge half asleep and unthinking, or in the melee of avoidance someone would find themselves catapulted out of the doorway. There then followed a farce of Keystone Cop proportions, as Spence chased his unwilling quarry relentlessly around the outside of the coop, whilst the others stood poised in the doorway, timing their escape to the second. As Spence whizzed past on each subsequent circuit, another chicken would jump down and make the dash to the drinker, narrowly avoiding the pursued and her pursuer as they sped past. Invariably, before completion of the fifth circuit Spence would get his girl, and she would finally walk away, fluffing up her feathers with a shudder or two, looking a little flustered and, with a brief backward glance, vowing not to be the first one out the following morning.

It seemed that we had got the new incubator just in time. After dark, when it was infinitely easier to distinguish shapes and movements through the thick shells of the goose eggs, we candled the eggs again, apprehensive of what we might find. The bright light amazingly revealed that five out of the six eggs had live goslings. Not only that, but two of them had already pierced the membrane and had their beaks in the little air sac at one end, which meant they were likely to hatch within the next 48 hours! We had been led to believe that as the eggs were from a large breed of goose, incubation would be nearer to 35 days than 30, but we were only on day 28, so ours would probably hatch much sooner than we'd expected.

The next morning I was up extra early to let the ducks out of their house. I wasn't going to commit to letting them out this early *every* morning, but as this had been their first night in their new quarters, I felt allowances could be made. The pen was still a quagmire, but inside of the duck house, as they had been without water to play with overnight, it was pleasantly dry. Cleaning took just a few minutes, in stark comparison to the hour or so it had been taking when they were in the garage. Today the ducks seemed to be less impulsive and keen to make amends for the messy state of affairs they'd found themselves in the day before. The clay mud that had coated their feathers the previous night had now dried, and they emerged from the house a pale grey in colour, with vaguely yellow downy tufts on their heads and tails. Turns were taken to paddle in the 'stream' and they sort out the driest patches on which to snooze between their regular feeding frenzies. The day, thankfully, did turn out to be a lot drier, just as the forecasters had predicted, which helped hugely, though the weathermen on all channels were promising horrendous rain and wind, and even possibly snow, for the next day, which was not a happy prospect in any shape or form.

On cleaning out the chickens that morning, I found two broken eggs on the floor of the coop, which was most frustrating. At least the shells seemed reasonably hard, which was something, but I was at a loss as to what to do to encourage these two birds to lay in the nest boxes where their eggs wouldn't get stepped on and trashed. The golf balls were obviously not convincing these two, so a new strategy was needed. I vowed to get up earlier still the next day, to let them out. Maybe they felt intimidated by the others, and unable to cross the coop to the nest boxes. By letting everyone out early, the two early birds would get a chance to use the facilities in private. It was a theory I hoped was worth the effort of leaving my nice warm bed on what was predicted to be one of the foulest mornings we'd encountered since our arrival, if the forecasters were to be believed.

The forecasters *were* right. The wind tore at the collar of my raincoat as I made my way down to the chicken pen at the unearthly hour of 6.30am, and tiny hailstones stung my face as I fumbled with the ties that held the gate to the electric fence secure. I must have been mad! As I opened the door of the coop to surprised stares from the incumbents, one shell-less egg was just landing in front of me, followed by a mad dash from every corner of the coop to sample the delicious offering. I quickly wiped it up with some straw and sawdust, not wanting anyone to get a taste for eggs, as this could escalate the problem considerably. Further research was obviously required.

After trawling the internet at length once more, I discovered that soft shelled eggs were actually quite a common problem. Several new theories were found, from a lack of Vitamin D (with our recent weather a definite possibility) to every hen being physically different and some needing more calcium than others, which would explain why only two seemed to have the problem, whilst others produced excellent eggs with tough shells. The solution appeared to rest with a product from all good poultry suppliers that you added to the water, just a couple of drops at a time. This should, according to the customer reviews, solve the problem very quickly by giving them the extra kick of calcium they needed. It was certainly worth a shot, so I ordered some immediately.

The weather remained stormy all day, which resulted in a chocolate cake, filled and topped with butter icing, spotless bathrooms and even time to read my book (Jeanine McMullen's 'A Country Smallholding'). Meanwhile our first gosling was slowly working its way out of its egg, with a lot of 'chuntering' in the process. The high pitched calls could even be heard two rooms away. By 8pm the process was complete and he (though Brian was convinced it was female owing to the constant chuntering) lay bedraggled, wet and exhausted in the incubator. Heart-warmingly, the prostrate little bundle continued to call, encouraging his siblings to join him, and we could hear their muffled but eager responses. At bedtime, we transferred the hatchling to the brooder and hoped there would be more goslings out by the morning. Progress was slow though and it was three days before we had the a full complement of four babies.

Never having hatched geese before, we didn't fully appreciate the significance of the mobility issues two of our new babies were having. We just presumed that their staggering about and the strange shuffling along on bottoms with legs splayed out to the sides, was the result of them being very young. However, when there was no improvement 24 hours later, my concerns led me to investigate it further online. Goslings, it transpired, commonly suffer something called 'splayed leg', and apparently it is vital to provide them with a good grippy floor. I laid an old towel on the floor of the brooder, which proved an effective solution. I then 'hobbled' the two babies that were struggling. This involved putting an elastic band, twisted in the middle, just above their hocks, to hold their legs closer together. This worked really well, when they didn't pull it off, though it changed their centre of balance and to start with they staggered more than ever, falling head first into each other. Very soon though, they got used to the change and actually managed to stand using the hobbles. It was recommended that you leave the hobbles on for a few days, and if warm enough to get the goslings outside on grass for some walking practise. This was all really good advice and by the next day the goslings were walking normally and even getting up to mischief. We did however, have one gosling that was still struggling in the incubator. It had needed a considerable amount of help out of the egg when it still hadn't hatched two days after the others. We'd had one gosling die in the egg, having made it as far as breaking through to the air sac, and we didn't want a repeat of this. But when I eventually managed to help this one emerge from the egg over 24 hours later, it was clear that it was not really quite ready to hatch yet, as it had not fully absorbed the yolk and was still attached via its umbilical cord. I left it in the incubator whilst it slept and continued to absorb its yolk, and the following day transferred it to the brooder in the lounge. Progress was slow, and it really seemed to struggle to balance, regularly toppling onto its beak and staggering head long into the side of the box. This caused a great deal of interest from both the cat and the dog, who couldn't work out whether it was a tasty snack or a threat to security, respectively. But before long the gosling was able to join the others in the pen in the garage. It was evident though, that our first born gosling was developing, at best, a mischievous streak, and at worst, a nasty side, and we started to refer to him as 'The Bully'. He seemed intent on pulling the tail feathers of the others, particularly those of our little invalid, and the evidence was glaringly obvious, as three of the goslings sported wet backs and tails where they had been grabbed, whilst 'the bully' remained completely dry. Of course this could just be over zealous 'friendly' preening, but it has to be said some of the tugs looked jolly rough. This didn't bode well and I started to imagine the problems I might have with this fella as he reached adulthood, and considered the merits of arming myself with a big stick.

Meanwhile, the ducks were getting used to their outdoor run, and despite the biting east wind and heavy showers, they insisted on taking in the view from the icy waters of the 'stream' or sitting in the sheet of liquid mud they had created; this despite having the use of a very serviceable and comfortably dry duck house. In fact, so reluctant were they to use the house, we were forced to slip and slide around the pen trying to catch each individual duck and physically place them inside when it came to bedtime; that is *I* slipped and slid whilst Brian held the door (himself having a bad back of course). This farce continued, until, miraculously, on the third night we beat our way through the storm to the duck pen to find all but three ducks already in the house! Convinced that on seeing us they would all re-emerge from the house to play our usual little game of catch, we were amazed, and highly relieved, to see these last three turn round and take themselves off to bed before we had even reached the gate! We were stunned, but very grateful.

Any hopes that this might be the new bedtime trend however, were sadly dashed - it had just been a one-off - and there followed many, many nights where we continued to slip and slide around the duck pen in an effort to persuade our ducks to bed. And as the rain kept on falling, often in bucketfuls, the pen became deeper and deeper in liquid mud, making the process still more hazardous. Adjustments were needed, and I decided that the positioning of a few short lengths of plastic piping under the base boards and netting of the pen on the downward side should do the trick, allowing the excess water to drain away instead of puddling. Well that was the theory, but nothing seemed to solve the problem totally, not even spreading the area with grass clippings when I cut the lawn, though this strategy did seem to bind the mud together to some degree. We longed for the weatherman to forecast a period of dry weather, so much so that we became ridiculously obsessed with seeing every forecast at breakfast, lunch and tea, and hung on every small ray of hope.

7.Geese

The problem of feather pecking in the goslings' run continued, and it was soon evident that we needed to separate 'The Bully' from the rest, before some serious damage was caused, particularly to our weakest gosling, who seemed to have become the main target. I set up a piece of board to create two enclosures, one end having the heat lamp and most of the goslings, whilst the other end had the 'electric chicken' and the troublemaker.

I had read on the internet that you could buy a spray that would stop feather pecking and luckily our local agricultural merchant had some. As we were going through town, on our way to look at some second hand poultry equipment that a friend of a friend was getting rid of, we picked some up.

Arriving at the farm, it was clear that it had once been a very big enterprise, and there were stacks of poultry houses and pens lining the driveway. There was also a huge metal barn, filled with everything you could imagine needing for poultry, from drinkers to egg boxes. They had, in fact, housed 500 chickens and sold rare breeds very successfully, until the novelty wore off. We had gone with the intention of buying an electric poultry net for our goslings, but we came away with two huge bales of sawdust, a large field drinker, and a hatcher as well. We were also told that the expensive anti-feather-pecking spray we'd just purchased wouldn't work, as the chap had only ever known one to work and it wasn't the one we had bought, which was frankly a tad dispiriting. However, he was right, as it turned out - the spray, if anything, encouraged more pecking as they seemed to like the taste!

Meanwhile, the little gosling seemed to be going downhill. He appeared very weak when we went into the garage the next morning, and was staggering aimlessly about. We had not yet actually seen him eat anything and knew we had to get some food down him pretty soon, if he was to stand any chance of surviving. With no syringe to hand, we improvised with the tube from a ball point pen and liquidised some chick crumbs with milk and warm water. This was pushed down the pen tube with a drill bit. Each tiny beak full needed to be washed down with water, so the gosling's beak was dipped into the drinker. Every hour throughout the day this process was repeated. By bedtime the poor bird was totally exhausted and we were unsure as to what we would find in the morning.

But in the morning, the gosling was still alive and even starting to show some signs of improvement. He was, though, still not taking the chick crumbs from the feeder, even when the others showed him what to do. Getting back on the internet over breakfast, I came across an article that recommended sprinkling the yolk of a hardboiled egg onto some chick crumbs, to encourage young chicks to start eating. Well we had plenty of eggs, so we gave it a try. It worked perfectly, and before long the little gosling was eating the chick crumbs just like the others. The relief was immense. Now we just had to solve the problem of feather pecking, as we couldn't keep 'The Bully' separated forever.

The solution came with the introduction of handfuls of grass to the pen; the idea being that the goslings become more intent on pecking the grass than each other. It was so simple and amazingly it worked. It seems that geese get bored very easily and need something to keep them entertained, even if it is only a pile of grass clippings. To start with we still separated 'The Bully' at night, when we couldn't keep an eye on him, but within a couple of days the goslings were together again and getting along just fine, much to our relief. It had been a steep learning curve raising geese, and we were only one week in.

We were now able to take a more relaxed approach with the goslings, and I don't know whether it was because we only had 4 goslings, or whether it is the way of geese (though this was contrary to all my past experience) but they seemed very keen on our company and would constantly follow us when we went into the garage. Their little feet would rapidly patter across the concrete floor, shadowing our every movement, running to whichever end of their pen we were nearest to. This became

66

even more comical when, they rushed to the far end of the pen, where a cardboard box rested on its side with the electric chicken inside making a cosy den, as occasionally one set of pattering feet would run into the box, instead of past it to the end of the pen like his companions, and a small head would reappear shortly afterwards, peering out of the box, head cocked to one side and eyes glazed with the confusion of finding himself all alone. Unlike the ducklings, who had run away from us most of the time (maybe they had an inkling as to our plans for them), the goslings ran towards us and genuinely seemed pleased to see us, pleading with us to give them a fuss or come and entertain them. This of course brought a dilemma; being friends sounds like a good idea, knowing how aggressive geese can be, but if you're thinking of eating them, you really don't want to get too attached. However, these little bundles of fluff that looked up to us with their appealing little faces and mischievous characters, were hard to resist, and nicknames (rightly or wrongly) became attributed. There was The Bully (of course), Titch (our little struggler) and The Twins (who were identical in every way and indistinguishable from each other); we're not very imaginative when it comes to names.

Things were briefly looking up in the chicken pen too, and at long last we had five chickens laying hard-shelled eggs. Most eggs were not up to proper size yet, but we were getting several larger ones, which turned out to be double-yolkers, apparently common when chickens first start laying. Buoyed up by this success, I decided to put my stall out by the gate, laden with my best half-dozen eggs, one or two herb plants I'd grown from seed and a couple of jars of raspberry jam. This was boosted by Brian adding his spare cauliflower and broccoli plants, also grown from seed. With blackboards facing up and down the lane, advertising our wares we sat back and waited excitedly for the sound of cars slowing down to buy. Our first sale came on the third day, and we didn't look back from that point really. I even had a local Welsh farmer come and tell me how lovely my lemon curd and jam was, and how his children and wife (who was a keen baker and W.I. member) couldn't get enough of it! It was good to know I was on the right track, though he did say that I was selling it too cheap, so there followed a minor price increase.

Of course, as soon as we started selling the eggs, some of the chickens went on strike and we went back to getting just 2 eggs a day. And more worryingly, we also had our first egg-bound chicken to deal with.

I noticed Meg sitting apart from the others, looking very fluffed up with half-closed eyes. At first I thought she was just tired, but then realised that her eyes were probably shutting as she concentrated on pushing the egg that was obviously stuck. I rang the breeder who had sold the chickens to us, to see if she had any advice.

Soon after, I was to be found sat in front of the television in the lounge, with the afflicted chicken in a bowl of warm water at my feet! Amazingly, she seemed to find it relaxing and she sat mesmerised by 'The National Lottery – In It To Win It'. After 20 minutes I popped her in a cardboard box whilst she dried off, and about half an hour before dark I took her back to the coop. As I popped her through the door, the troublesome, and as it turned out soft-shelled, egg was expelled immediately onto the floor of the coop. Thankfully, by the following morning Meg was her normal self again, and another crisis had successfully been averted.

~

The smallholding was expanding nicely, with chickens, ducks and goslings, when one Sunday afternoon the boys arrived. George and Oliver were two little Shetland ponies looking for some fresh grazing, and whose owners lived just down the lane, in the village. We, of course, were only too pleased for something to graze our overgrown field, so an electric pony fence was erected and the boys released. There was just one problem: as the grass was quite tall and the ponies quite short, it was often tricky to spot them (and indeed, for *them* to spot each other!) We frequently were victim to misguided concern as to the whereabouts of the ponies, and palpitations at the prospect of the boys having escaped from the field entirely, until a head was lifted momentarily and we'd breathe a sigh of relief. They seemed very happy to munch their way through brambles, reeds and rough grassy tussocks, whilst playing a somewhat enforced version of hide and seek, and we could at last forget about the neglected state of the field for a while, whilst the ponies did their best to bring it under control.

The sun was even shining, at long last, after what had seemed like eons of wet weather. In fact the weather looked set for a fairly dry and sunny week, which was good because we had several jobs that had been waiting for just such a break in the weather. One job that was looming, was the dispatching of the ducks, and we decided that Friday would be D-day.

As ducks pine for each other, and get very stressed if separated from their friends, the only way to dispatch them is to do them all on the same day; so this was going to be a major operation which called for some careful planning. Extra buckets were bought, the new freezer switched on a couple of days before and the temperature of the tea urn tested. This would be our first opportunity to try out the Whizbang Chicken Plucker that Jack had made for us. I just hoped it would hold together for the whole batch of ten ducks. There was both excitement and trepidation in the air. Whatever else happened, it was really important to us that the process was as calm and as efficient as possible, to prevent any undue stress for the birds.

Brian was chosen to 'do the deed' (something I'm afraid I didn't feel able to do myself). The dead bird would then need to be hung by its feet, on a hook suspended from one of the beams in the garage, where it would be bled. Then the bird would be dunked in the tea urn for a few seconds before being put in the chicken plucker for one minute. Then Brian would gut the bird before I bagged it up for the freezer. Well, that was the plan, and all the equipment was laid out in the garage the day before, with this in mind. However, as ever, things didn't quite go as we'd hoped.

Firstly, the ducks were bigger and stronger than we had anticipated, and Brian struggled to 'do the deed' on his own. It was evident that dispatching would be a two person job, and as I was the only other person available, that would have to be me. Despite my squeamishness I would have to step up to the mark. This I did, and although my insides were churning, I just wanted the process to be as quick as possible for each bird, so I got on with it.

Once the bird was dead, I had no problem with the rest of the process. However, we were to discover further glitches in our plan. The first bird was dipped in the hot water to loosen the feathers and the Whizbanger switched on. But the weight of the bird was just too much for the machine, and despite some tweaking, the motor could not manage to fling the carcass around as it should; well actually, not at all! We had to revert to traditional methods and get hand plucking. And to add insult to injury, we had obviously mistimed it with regard to the growth of pin feathers, which were coming through in huge abundance on most of the birds. The only way I could see to remove these was with tweezers, one at a time. It was going to be a very long day!

I had sent a message to Jack, reporting the problems we'd had with the Whizbanger, and by lunchtime there was an email from him suggesting an adjustment that we could make, that would speed the motor up. This we did and we decided to try the Whizbanger again with the next bird.

This time the Whizbanger turned fine with the weighty bird, but our joy was sadly short-lived. As we watched the duck spinning wildly around the blue barrel, it seemed to be shrinking before our very eyes! Extremities proceeded to fly off in all directions, feet, legs, neck, whilst we both hung on grimly to the violently shaking machine, in an effort to prevent it shuffling into the nearby ditch. We stopped the machine, and yes, most of the feathers *had* been removed, but there appeared to be something seriously amiss with the shrunken corpse that had now come to a halt with a thud in the bottom of the barrel. The full extent of the damage only came to light once Brian started to gut the poor unfortunate. Every single bone in its body was broken, and following the removal of its insides, it now was pretty much flat. It was clear that we would have to go back to the drawing board with the Whizbanger. The duck was bagged and labelled, 'Whizbang Duck – watch out for broken bones!' and dispatched to the freezer.

By 7pm we still had two birds to pluck and another three to gut, but at least all the ducks had been humanely dispatched.

We were exhausted and the decision to pick up some fish and chips and call it a day was a very popular move. The rest would have to be finished the following day.

It was a truly pleasing sight to see such a pile of large ducks in the freezer, and we were pleasantly surprised at the weights which ranged from 5lb (Whizbang duck – well it *was* missing several of its extremities) to 7lb. One bird however didn't make it as far as the freezer, as it was whisked straight into the oven; we just couldn't wait to sample the taste of our first home-reared meat, and we weren't to be disappointed...the taste was simply delicious. We had got the fat content just right and the meat was so tender and tasty you really couldn't fault it. We *would* be repeating the process again – but not *too* soon. We needed time for our aching muscles and sore fingers to convalesce, and the duck run would need several months to recover from the vandalism of its previous inhabitants.

Over the next few weeks the 'stream' walls were rebuilt and reinforced, and the mud was topped with fresh soil before it was reseeded. A spell of hot sunny weather helped enormously, to erase the devastation and return the duck run to a useable state.

We had learnt some valuable lessons and our next production of ducks would see some important changes. Firstly we would hatch them a month later, so that we wouldn't have to keep them in the garage for quite so long - hopefully the weather would be warmer and not so wet. We would also dispatch them at 7 weeks, not 8, so as to avoid the growth of pin feathers. And we would definitely *not* be using the Whizbanger for processing the ducks!

~

As we approached the end of May, we suddenly seemed to be getting a steady five eggs a day, all with hard shells and all laid properly in the nest boxes provided. And a good job too, as it was becoming difficult to keep up with the demand for eggs at the gate. Why we had plumped for five hens and not six, I really don't know; it made filling egg boxes quite frustrating. So we decided to increase our flock by two. This figure was arrived at as we were told it was not a good idea to introduce one chicken on its own to an established flock, for fear of it being picked on. We also figured that we had just enough room for two more chickens in the existing coop.

I rang Sandra, our original supplier. Sadly, it turned out that she had just suffered a devastating daytime attack from a fox, and twenty-four of her birds had been killed, despite her husband being on hand to chase the culprit off. It was frightening to hear how the fox had continued to snatch at chickens as he was vehemently pursued, and eventually expelled from the yard. Sandra didn't have any Point of Lay hens left, but she did have some twelve-week old pullets she said we could have, and she agreed to hang onto them for a month, until she felt they would be able to cope with being introduced to the rest of the gang.

As it happened, we ended up with not two, but three, new girls – a sort of 'buy 2, get one free'! The extra chicken had a slightly deformed toe, but was otherwise perfectly fine, and not ones to turn down a freebie, we gladly took her on as well. With a slight readjustment of the perches we managed to squeeze a bit more space in the coop, so as to accommodate the extra arrival.

When the day came to pick up our three new girls, we arranged to collect them in the early evening; the theory being that you wait until the main flock have gone to bed, then you pop the new birds onto the perches next to them. Apparently, or so we were assured by Sandra, the existing birds are too comatose to notice what's going on, and by morning everybody is friends. This sounded all too simple to be true, but we went with it, being the novices that we were, and kept our fingers tightly crossed. As night fell and the main flock settled down to roost in the coop, we slid the three new birds (Milly, Molly and Mandy) quietly into the nest box. Spence, however, still had one eye open and was soon loudly alerting the whole coop as to the clandestine goings on. Thankfully though, as we closed the nest box lid again, quiet calm was restored. The ventilation holes were closed, so that it would be as dark as possible in the morning, to help prevent the interlopers being spotted before I could release them, and we tiptoed away.

72

The following morning I was up early to release the chickens. I nervously opened the coop door and out popped Spence, oversexed and ready for action as usual, followed by one of the older birds. An unsuspecting Milly then emerged, blinking in the morning sunshine and taking in her new surroundings, unaware of our cockerel's morning routine. Spence almost immediately jumped on her and I had to intervene to dissuade his advances. The older girls then chased her off to the edge of the run where she remained alone and somewhat despondent. So, not exactly friends yet then!

Having seen what had befallen their friend, Molly and Mandy needed more than a little gentle persuasion to exit the coop, and on doing so they too were treated to some cruel jibes and jabs, and banished to the outer reaches. Well, at least the three new girls had each other whilst the settling in process ran its course. I knew chickens could be cruel, but it is still rather sad to see your docile, homely chickens turn into vicious and spiteful bullies. Even my dear Alice, who is the friendliest chicken alive normally, had a bit of rough justice for the new girls.

The day rumbled on in much the same vein, with the indignant older girls snapping at the youngsters who, in an effort to avoid Spence's unwanted advances, sought shelter in the nest boxes. However, they were simply in the way when there was egg laying to be done, and feathers flew, accompanied by a great deal of swearing, for much of the day.

Ousted from the coop, and with the weather taking a miserable turn for the worse, Milly, Molly and Mandy huddled together in the middle of the run, bedraggled sad figures, as the rain hammered down, not daring to join their adversaries who sheltered comfortably beneath the coop.

In an attempt to offer some comfort, I braved the storm and propped an upturned wheelbarrow on a bucket, hoping that they would shelter beneath it. Nervous of being cornered however, they declined the opportunity to get out of the rain and remained rooted and exposed. It really was a miserable day for the new girls, and we still had bedtime to endure.

As the light began to fade at the end of a very long day, the older chickens were restless and constantly hopping in and out of the house, whilst the youngsters stuck to the edge of the run, trying to look unconcerned, but quite obviously anxious. As I stood by the gate observing the pitiful scenario, the rain started to fall again, doing little to help any of our dispositions. Eventually all the older girls were in the coop, and Milly, Molly and Mandy snuck under the coop; at least they were out of the rain. One after the other, the older chickens craned their necks through the open door to ascertain the whereabouts of the interlopers. However, being beneath the coop and out of view from those within, soon resulted in a loss of interest, and before long the best perches were occupied and just one bouncer left to guard the door. Thinking we would have to resort to popping the new girls in through the nest box again, when everyone had settled, Brian was on standby to help me. It would not be an easy job catching the sodden newcomers in the ensuing darkness. The rain now began to fall like stair-rods. We stood, hoods pulled over our heads, waiting to see what would happen. Then to our surprise Milly bravely (or perhaps stupidly) marched straight up the ramp, past the guard on the door and into the coop! We waited for it all to kick off, but there was not a sound, so we lingered some more, getting wetter and wetter. Before long, Mandy plucked up the courage to make her entrance. Meg came to the door and did her best to totally fill it, but Mandy just ducked her head and squeezed past. Again, there was no resulting commotion. Now that Molly was left on her own, she really didn't have much choice, and we didn't have to wait long before she too had made the perilous ascent to the top of the ramp. I closed the door and quietly whispered, 'Good night.'

Brian, not one to stand a moment longer in the rain than absolutely necessary, went off to feed the cat, or take up some other job that could be done in the comfort of a dry, warm house, and I stood listening to the chunterings issuing from the coop as everyone settled down for the night, rain cascading from my hood and down my frozen cheeks. Hopefully they would all emerge tomorrow, better acquainted and ready to accept each other, as this was all very exhausting, physically and emotionally - and not just for the chickens!

Five days later some improvement was evident, with Milly, Molly and Mandy managing to edge closer to one or two of the older girls without actually getting jabbed at by a hostile beak, but it was all still very tense. However, after several more days where egg production had dipped to three eggs, we seemed to be back to our normal five eggs, so we felt cautiously optimistic, and by the end of the week most of the swearing seemed to have greatly diminished. The newcomers had been allocated their place in the pecking order and they were in absolutely no doubt that they were at the bottom. An uneasy tolerance developed. In the mornings when I opened up the coop, the older girls would pile out first, whilst the youngsters held back making the most of any empty coop and my protective presence to fill up with feed. Once I had finished cleaning the coop, the older girls returned demanding absolute privacy for the important task of egg laying, and the youngsters wisely and rapidly vacated the premises.

There was great pride, and more than a little boastfulness, as each egg was produced; each hen loudly announcing its arrival to the whole valley as she emerged from the coop (which was very useful if you were waiting for an egg to cook with or complete a box to sell at the gate). Since the arrival of the newcomers, this egotistic gloating seemed to have escalated somewhat, and was, I felt, a tad insensitive, as the youngsters were yet to produce any eggs of their own.

As well as our laying chickens, our plan was to raise chickens 'for the table', but with the apparent demand for eggs so high, we decided to breed some more egg layers instead. We could eat the cockerels and keep the hens, and maybe try to sell a couple of point-of-lay (POL) hens online too.

Over the next few days we came up with a variety of possible figures, but eventually plumped for eight new layers and a couple of POLs. To get this we reckoned, as we could expect half to be cockerels and would need to allow for some not hatching, we'd need to put twenty eggs in the incubator.

With our existing birds, this would give us a total of sixteen laying hens and should result in a summer output of between twelve and sixteen eggs a day, pretty much doubling our sales at the gate, and even giving us some eggs for our own use too - something we'd not had for several weeks.

We then had three days when none of the eggs we put out sold, and we reconsidered our strategy - could we cope with sixteen eggs a day, if we didn't sell them? In the end however, we stuck with our decision and set twenty eggs in the incubator.

With the ducks no longer in the picture, I just had my chickens to look after, which freed up more of my time to get on with other jobs about the place. Brian was in charge of the goslings, as they were his idea in the first place, and once they were over the first few tricky days and eating properly, 'mucking out' became his responsibility. Brian, having, in my opinion, greatly underestimated how much work was involved when I had looked after the miscreant ducks, would surely now fully appreciate my heroic contribution and hard labour, as he now took his turn with the livestock, but of course, as soon as he took over the care of the goslings, they were rapidly moved outside during the day, reducing the workload considerably!

Thinking about it I could hardly have been surprised, as I remembered the point when I returned to work after having the children, and Brian (who worked from home) became responsible for doing the washing up each day. In less than a month we were the proud owners of our very first dishwasher!

At just three weeks of age the goslings were to be predominantly fed on grass, with just a few pellets of feed when they came into their shed at night. With this in mind, the erection of an electric fence around the blackcurrant bushes on the hillside, close to the chalet, became a priority. This was not an easy job with all the lumps and bumps in the ground, not to mention the steep incline. Luckily, we had been advised by the chap we had bought the second-hand fence from, to use strips of waterproof membrane from the builders' merchant to put under the netting, in order to prevent the grass from growing and shorting out the fence. This worked really well, and I wished I'd known about this earlier, when I had been setting up the chicken run. It was a good insulator and even where the netting rested horizontally on the membrane, there was still no shorting. As the goslings were still a bit on the small side, we also tied a string across the enclosure with some CDs flapping on it, to discourage any interest there might be from Buzzards and Red Kites.

We thought the goslings would be delighted with all this space to run around in, but when we introduced them to the wide open spaces of their run, they were rather overwhelmed by it all. Their initial anxiety was only added to when, inevitably, they touched the electric fence, sending them squealing to hide under the skirts of the currant bushes, where they recuperated in the shadows until they felt strong enough to embark upon any further tentative explorations.

As bedtime approached, the goslings were ushered back down the hill to the tin shed which stood at the edge of the lawn, and which had become their new night quarters. Of course, as they left the confines of the run, through the gate in the now deactivated electric fence, the goslings had to cross the membrane, and understandably they were reluctant to do this. A great deal of encouragement was needed to persuade them across it, especially when they were in the early stages of learning that the fence was best avoided. Most opted to make a dash for it, obviously believing that if they were quick it would hurt less, but one of 'the twins' adopted a more athletic two-feet-together jump, which he employed each and every crossing, clearing it in fine style, but always after a brief hesitation, in which I imagined him to be calculating the distance, possible trajectory and required effort to ensure a safe landing on the other side.

As they grew, the geese continued to love our company and whenever they heard our voices in the garden they would run full pelt down the hill towards us, often struggling to stop before they hit the electric fence! Regularly, we would take a cup of tea up to the chalet and sit on the 'veranda' watching the goslings, who would hurry across from the little field shelter that I'd made for them, to flop as close as they could to where we were sitting. Their gait, as they got bigger, was becoming more of a waddle, and the development of large baggy pouches of skin around the tops of their thighs, only added to the comic effect as they made a bee-line for us, like a group of enthusiastic boy scouts in Baden Powell shorts (of the Eric Morecombe variety).

~

The end of May saw a flurry of visitors and for a fortnight little work got done on the smallholding. I was catapulted into what seemed like endless hours of cooking and loading and unloading the dishwasher. Typically, with the arrival of visitors, the weather, which had been incredibly hot and sunny for days (so much so that we couldn't bear to work in it, and had been rising early to get our jobs done before the sun had reached its full heat, and had worked late in the evening as the sun sank behind the wood at the top of the hill), now turned 'changeable' and a lot cooler. We went from temperatures above normal to those below the norm, in the space of just a few hours, giving us a few new dilemmas to test our patience. Visitors, we often found, enjoyed joining in with chores such as stoking bonfires or collecting eggs, or were happy to sit in the sun with a newspaper, walk in the woods or visit the coast. But wet weather was always a challenge when it came to entertaining visitors. The shops locally were limited, and once the small stately home near Aberaeron had been seen, there was little else to do when it rained. Normally of course, we just kept going, suitably dressed in waterproofs, or we'd work in the garage making useful additions to chicken coops or goose enclosures, or prick out seedlings in the greenhouse, none of which really tends to appeal to visitors. So, unless they are the type of visitors that like a good game of Monopoly or cards, sadly the TV is the only option left. Luckily, with the Queen's Diamond Jubilee celebrations in full swing there was plenty to see on this particular occasion, and we were thankful.

8. Poultry Concerns

In our first few months at Nantcoed we had endured a seemingly endless amount of wet weather. However, it had eventually given way to several welcome weeks of very dry weather and gloriously hot sunny days, resulting in a hosepipe ban in many counties of the UK (though not Wales unsurprisingly). In June though, we saw the return of the wet stuff. The most torrential rain and wild storms for over twenty years hit the district of Aberystwyth, just forty miles to the north of us. Flash flooding caused havoc in the town's superstores, and caravan parks were completely washed away overnight.

The River Teifi at the bottom of the hill looked likely to threaten the village, gushing through the old stone bridge at an unprecedented rate, and Brian and I took a walk down to the shop to assess the situation.

It all appeared safe for now, but even our sweet babbling stream had become a torrent, which rushed angrily down the side of the lawn just feet from the front door. Although we had some brighter mornings, the following week saw yet more heavy deluges, and still there was no prospect of any improvement. For once though the rain clouds were not limited to Wales, and most of the UK suffered similar weather. In fact after just a week, most of the reservoirs were close to full again and most of the hosepipe bans were but a distant memory...so much for 'Flaming June'!

It felt as though we had had a lot more than our fair share of rain since we'd moved to Wales, and I must say spirits were rock-bottom. Not least because the wet weather had escalated the slug problem, and Brian declared that every single lettuce he had nurtured in the cold frame was now lost to the 'f***ing slugs'. Indeed, despite my efforts to cheer him with the news that there were sparks issuing from the electric fence due to one well-fried slug being reduced to a puddle of slime, his mood remained mournfully black.

Even I was becoming fed up with the constant downpours, and my normal optimism and good humour was beginning to wane with the nagging notion that this might just be how it is in Wales, and that it may not get any better! This was not helped by mischievous comments from the locals, who took great delight in winding us up with stories about May being the only decent month of the year in these parts, and not to expect much more in the way of summer for another 11 months. We retired to the lounge and lit the log burner, whilst the wind rattled the chimney and blew the chickens' petticoats inside out. The geese, although they had their lovely field shelter, chose to sit out in the open, seemingly oblivious to the torrential rain being hurled horizontally into their faces. Expert advice had stressed the importance of 'protecting geese from sun, rain and wind at all times', but our geese were obviously made of tougher stuff, luckily, and had actually only used the shelter for protection from the heat of the sun. One wondered how much use they would get out of it in the long term!

The geese had so far done an excellent job of keeping the grass trimmed between the blackcurrant bushes, so much so that we needed to rest it for a week and allow it to recover a little. We decided to allow them to 'free-range' on the lawn, as we were to be home for several days and could keep an eye on them. Geese, however, are prolific producers of excrement; grass and water go in at one end and muck simultaneously drops out of the other, with absolutely no effort whatsoever. And so we regularly found ourselves tip-toeing between dollops whenever we ventured further than the patio. To prevent the geese from fouling the patio itself, we had lined up a variety of obstacles along the edge; some small wooden fencing that I'd made from strips of pallet wood, which stood no taller than 30cm, some solid lengths of plywood and the watering can. Eventually I hoped to procure enough wood to make sufficient small fencing strips to reach the whole length of the patio, but in the meantime we had to make do. The watering can proved less effective than we'd hoped however, and this was for two reasons. Firstly, the geese found they could duck under the spout to enter the restricted area, much to their obvious delight and our dismay, and secondly, it proved to be a draw rather than a deterrent, as they vied for the chance to dip their beaks and long necks deep into the water. Sometimes two would reach in together, and then a struggle would ensue as two heads attempted to withdraw through the small opening at the same time; geese are not well acquainted with the notion of taking turns, which frequently led to some highly entertaining situations. Geese in fact, just do whatever they feel like, whenever they feel like doing it. They have no spatial awareness whatsoever, or social graces it would seem. If they have chosen a place to sit, it is of no consequence if that spot is already occupied – they just sit on top of the present occupant. They also only walk in straight lines, regardless of any obstacles or other geese lying in their path; they simply climb over them (going round is *never* an option). This of course made them extremely good fun to watch, and many hours were spent giggling at their antics.

The geese, now being free-range, could of course explore areas thus far unconquered, much to the annoyance of all the other incumbents of our smallholding. For one, our little black cat, Dot, did not appreciate their bumbling interference as she sat statue-still in the long grass, patiently poised to pounce on an unsuspecting mouse or vole emerging from a tussock. Four large and curious geese did nothing for her catch-rate or disposition; her irritation palpable, she stalked off to find a less accessible corner of the field, where she could hunt in peace.

The chickens too, had their problems. They had generally ignored the geese up to this point, even though their pens were just a couple of metres apart. However, when these large birds appeared at the open gate of the chicken pen, nibbling absent-mindedly at the guy ropes which held the electric fence taut, they could not be ignored and an indignant Spence marched down the hill, ready to give them a piece of his mind. However, as he got nearer he appeared to freeze mid-strut, one foot lingering with uncertainty in mid-air. Having got close enough now to fully appreciate the height and breadth of these miscreants, he was clearly having second thoughts, and after a brief re-evaluation, he tactically swivelled back the way he'd come, glancing briefly over his shoulder to check that he'd not been followed. Meanwhile, to add insult to injury, the girls seemed completely unperturbed by the group and were happy to peck right up to the fence where the geese had decided to set up temporary camp. The geese it seemed were just as interested in the chickens, and they would regularly line up along the electric fence, all facing towards the coop as if settled on the sofa in front of their favourite TV soap.

Despite the intimidation experienced by the other residents, it was also good to see that the geese had so far shown no aggression towards *us*. They had stretched out their long necks towards Storm, our dear, placid German Shepherd, as he passed them on his way down the field, but with his failing eyesight he was seemingly oblivious to their gestures, and the geese were generally left feeling ineffectual and somewhat deflated. They were actually, not as tough as they tried to make out, as I discovered one morning when I passed them on my way down to feed the chickens. As we appeared to be friends, I bent down and gently wrapped my arm around 'The Bully', giving him an affectionate little hug, only to be instantly deafened by a wail of utter panic as he struggled free from my embrace and rapidly sort to put a safe distance between us.

What we needed now was some sunshine to bring the Elderflowers out. I had collected everything else we needed to make Elderflower cordial, and now I just needed the key ingredient. Elderflower cordial is a refreshing summer drink, and I was determined to get some in the cold store. It also fills the house with the most wonderful aroma imaginable, whilst it steeps for a couple of days in a tea-towel covered bucket. When the sun did eventually appear, it was to be just a brief encounter, so the opportunity was grabbed without hesitation. However, when it came to it, finding enough elder bushes to muster the twenty flower heads I needed for even one batch of cordial was proving tricky. We had some along our own hedgerows, but not quite enough, so I decided to widen my search, and set off on my mountain bike (a wonderfully inspired gift from my work colleagues when I 'retired', to replace the old 'sit-up-and-beg' bike that they had taken such delight in ridiculing over the years, and on which, in my absence one day, they had hung a sign offering it for sale to the first comer for just 50p). I peddled up the hill and through the 300 acre community woodland that ran along the ridge above our house, in search of the elusive flower heads. After cycling over three miles and, incredibly, only spotting one elder bush (completely inaccessible and perilously perched on the edge of a deep ravine) I had to admit defeat and return home empty handed. The remaining elderflowers were eventually supplied by Brian, who had an errand to run on the far side of the valley, and who arrived home triumphantly, with a carrier bag held aloft and a big grin on his face.

Things in the chicken run remained strained, even by the end of June, with the new girls still not fully accepted by the older girls. Bedtime was becoming a long drawn-out affair as the youngsters tried their best to get past the bouncer on the door each night, but often they just couldn't pluck up the courage to face yet another pecking, and would settle for sleeping under the coop. I would then have to lift them up and sneak them into the coop by way of the nest boxes. With the weather showing no let up, this often meant prolonged periods of standing in the rain.

During the day the youngsters were fine, keeping themselves to themselves and out of trouble most of the time, but night-time was always problematic. Not only that, but I was having to get up at 6.30am to let them all out, before any arguments kicked-off. With all this stress, I felt sure the youngsters would never come into lay, which, after all, was the whole point of having the new girls. I made my mind up to solve the problem once and for all, and I sketched out some plans on the back of an old envelope for a 'granny annexe' and ordered the wood I needed. Within 2 days it was complete, balanced on the wheelbarrow and being wobbled across the field in the pouring rain. We positioned it to the side of the main coop, with its door facing south and away from the main entrance. There was great excitement in the chicken run as the new extension arrived and was manoeuvred into place (with the ever-present geese looking on, of course). Within a short space of time Spence had cautiously climbed the ramp, had a look around and declared the annexe 'officially open'. Others had poked their beaks in and had a nose about too, including Milly, Molly and Mandy. As bedtime approached, the old girls and Spence went through their now normal routine of keeping the youngsters out of the main coop, whilst the youngsters tried fruitlessly to gain entry. But when Bossy Flossie came out and gave her final warning before retiring to bed, the youngsters, thankfully gave up on the main coop and climbed the ramp to the annexe, settling down for their first peaceful night since they'd arrived. It was such a relief all round.

The next day everyone emerged fully refreshed and ready to face the day. There was continued interest in the new annexe by the old girls, and it was fully inspected again and again by all, whilst the new girls kept sensibly out of the way. Even when the rain came down in stair rods the youngsters did not venture inside the new extension, but huddled under a large but totally inadequate weed. Presumably they feared being trapped in the annexe, if one of the others should follow them in, so between showers I set up another little shelter for them, with a plank of wood and a couple of large logs.

By the following morning, dear Alice had decided that the nest box in the 'granny annexe' needed testing out properly, and she settled herself for a bit of egg laying. This was not in the plan; I had hoped to provide a refuge for the youngsters to lay their eggs, not more options for the already spoilt older girls. However, on reflection, maybe Alice's egg would help to give the new girls an idea of what was to be expected of them.

Meanwhile we had sixteen new chicks in the garage, who would, in time, form a new laying flock. We could not believe how tiny these babies were, and at first considered whether or not they were stunted in some way. Of course we had been used to seeing the huge ducklings and even 'huger' goslings that we'd hatched recently, so ping-pong ball sized chicks seemed miniscule in comparison. The actual hatch was much more straight-forward than either the ducks or the geese (thankfully), with all but one chick making it out of the egg independently. As we were relative novices, we were unable to distinguish male from female at this stage, but hoped for at least eight hens. Any extras we hoped to test the market with and sell as POLs (Point of Lays). If there proved a demand, we might even consider breeding some just to sell on. Any cockerels of course, would be heading for the freezer.

This also threatened to be the direction in which Spence was heading, as he had become particularly aggressive of late. If I was feeling generous, I might imagine his mood was just as a result of the upset caused by the arrival of the new girls and the 'granny annexe', which he now seemed intent on establishing as *his* territory. But it was hard to be generous when he seemed more and more intent on attacking me, especially when I collected the eggs, and it was getting to the point where I now needed to take the broom in with me each time, so that I could protect myself. We had been told that Light Sussex cockerels had a reputation for being more aggressive than their Buff counterparts, and this was looking like a distinct possibility.

9. Charmed Chickens

July started as June had finished – wet.

With a wealth of friends and family planning to visit over the coming weeks, we were praying for an upturn in the weather. The hope of treating our guests to balmy walks along the beach, a boat trip out to see the dolphins, or even just a relaxing afternoon on the patio, taking in the view with a cup of tea and some homemade cake (or maybe a glass of something stronger) seemed frankly remote.

The summer was going down in the record books as the wettest since records began, and there was no prospect of an improvement. With St. Swithen's Day approaching fast, everyone was intent on seizing the slightest positive note in the weather forecast, in order to avoid the prospect of another forty days of rain!

However, our first visitors of the month, my parents, in stark contrast to their last visit, were this time fortunate to encounter a significant amount of dry weather, and even a spot of sunshine, during their three day visit. We managed to have a much-longed-for paddle along the beach, eat our lunch *al fresco* at one of the cafes in New Quay, and scoff ice creams in Aberaeron, before the heavy showers put pay to any further outdoor activities.

Not long after waving farewell to my parents, I was back to the essentials around the smallholding, such as checking the electric fences for places where they might be shorting. The most likely cause for this was generally yet another slug being fried into a puddle of slime (and Lord knows, we had an abundance of slugs!) Making my way back towards the house to fetch the spade, I could hear voices at the gate, one of which was Brian's, and being the nosey sort of person I am, I went to see who he was talking to. As I got nearer, I could see the bright glow of a high-visibility jacket and what looked like a police car. My immediate thought was that my stall by the gate had fallen fowl of the local by-laws or was causing some kind of distraction hazard. With an excess of lettuces, eggs, redcurrants and other bits and pieces, there was plenty on the little stall. Although I had investigated the laws relating to the selling of eggs from the gate, and knew we met with all the regulations, I was less certain about the sales of elderflower cordial that I had recently deposited there... and now the POLICE were here!

Luckily, as it turned out, one of the officers had spotted the elderflower cordial, and having a great love for the stuff, had insisted on stopping so that he could buy some. Phew! There then followed plenty of chat and banter over the garden gate, which is always nice, and definitely preferable to being issued with any kind of summons or being arrested for having a hazardously eye-catching stall. I returned to my slug hunt.

The war on slugs was in fact poised to escalate to a whole new level. Brian had finally, in his desperation to put a halt to the destruction being wreaked in his vegetable plot, invested in some nematodes, and when the weather was right he was going to release them amongst his carrots and cabbages. He had ordered them by phone and been told by the girl that on arrival they must be stored in the fridge. She had also warned that they had to be applied to wet soil and be kept wet for at least the next two weeks. He assured her, with absolute certainty, that this would not be a problem!

We had also been given, by a friend, a homeopathic solution to try called Helix Tosta (or Burnt Snail) which could be sprayed onto the leaves of plants you wanted to protect. These potential remedies arrived not a moment too soon, as Brian had just lost another whole tray of young lettuce plants overnight, and the slugs seemed to be multiplying at an alarming rate. Speed was of the essence.

But this of course is Brian we're talking about, and he likes to get things 'just right'. So he waited a couple of weeks for warmer weather in order to maximise the success of the nematodes. In the meantime though, yet more leaves were turned to lace or digested entirely, leaving some of the raised beds resembling doyley plantations and others completely devoid of any green shoots whatsoever.

Then at long last, the weather forecasters started talking about a much more settled spell of weather, and even sunshine! The jet stream, it seemed, was going back to its proper position north of Scotland, and you could almost feel the whole country holding its breath in anticipation, hardly daring to believe that the long awaited summer was about to arrive.

The nematodes were at last released to do their stuff, though of course with the warmer, drier weather, came the need for a watering can, to ensure the correct conditions were adhered to.

~

At almost four weeks of age our new, homebred chicks were living a charmed life. Firstly, Dot (who had recently honed her bird catching skills with the assistance of one very unfortunate Great-Tit just that morning) had got into the garage, where the chicks were being kept in their pen made from off-cuts of wood and sturdy cardboard boxes. How long she was in there for, nobody knows, but Brian was the first to realise half way through the evening, that we had not seen the cat for a while and went to check the outbuildings. How she got into the garage was baffling, as we had lived in dread of such an occurrence and had consequently been super-diligent in our efforts to keep the garage door firmly shut. In fact, on more than one occasion I had found myself locked in the garage, after Brian, not realising I was in there and discovering the bolt pulled back, had slid it closed to prevent just such intruders. Luckily I discovered that I could swing both doors open and make my escape, by drawing the two huge, heavy bolts that held the adjoining door firmly in place. Initially I had tried shouting and banging on the door, but Brian was invariably out of ear-shot up the garden... or so he said.

Amazingly, on this occasion Dot appeared to have ignored the chicks completely and they had miraculously survived unscathed. Considering how the chicks were inclined to flutter up onto the top of the boards, from which they could then launch themselves into all sorts of adventures around the garage, the temptation must have been excruciating and I can't imagine how she contained herself.

It seemed an opportune time to move the sixteen chicks outside. I rigged up some garden netting to cordon off a small area in what was going to be the new chicken pen on the lower field. I had already erected an electric poultry fence and started to clear the ground, and there was a new double-ended chicken house, that I'd made from wood from the local tip. The biggest danger to the young birds would probably be the crows and buzzards, so I stretched some netting across the top of the coop and over the edges of the electric fence. Hopefully this canopy would also prevent the chicks from fluttering up and over the fence.

On release into this new run, the chicks were utterly delighted, and they ran in all directions, bumping into each other as they criss-crossed and fluttered from one side to the other. I didn't put the electric fence on at first, as I thought it might be a step too far for ones so small. I watched them carefully for some time, to ensure that all was well. Then, just as I was about to walk back up to the house, one chick and then another walked straight through the squares in the electric fence, to peck at the obviously greener grass on the other side. Picking the escapees up and popping them back over the netting, I turned the electric fence on, and stood and watched again. Several chicks attempted a push for freedom, each suffering a short, sharp zap which sent them squealing under the coop, fluffed up and sorry for themselves, but there were no further escapees. All seemed to be well now, so I returned to the house.

I checked on the chicks regularly throughout the afternoon and evening, and they seemed happy, and safely contained. They even looked as though they'd be fine to sleep in their new coop overnight, meaning that the potentially time-consuming process of catching them all and transferring them between their run and the garage each evening, and back again in the morning, could thankfully be avoided.

However, when Brian went out soon after 8pm that evening, to bring the geese down from the top field for their evening feed, he was soon back waving his arms at me from the other side of the patio doors. Quite a few of the chicks had somehow got out and were wandering all over the garden, completely oblivious to the danger they could be in. Although Dot was inside, snoozing on one of the dining room chairs, there were foxes to worry about of course, and several feral cats that often came down to our fields from the woods. In deed just half an hour after this incident, one such cat walked straight past the patio doors!

As we approached the rebel chicks, wondering how on earth they could have escaped, they calmly, and rather magically, walked straight back through the electrified netting, totally untouched. These chicks obviously had more brains than they had first been given credit for, and had worked out that if they walked through without touching the sides of the squares, they could totally avoid being zapped – either that or they were just very lucky!

We were now back to square one, and all the chicks were gathered up, counted and returned to their pen in the garage. We would have to try again in a week, when hopefully they would be too big to try the same trick.

Four days later, after further adjustments, including the replacement of the netting over the chick pen (which was a nightmare to crawl beneath when opening or shutting the coop) with a number of CDs hung on fishing line (as it turned out, at a perfect height to garrotte me), we moved the chicks out permanently to their new run. They were getting too big to do anything else really, and we needed the space in the garage for the imminent arrival of a second batch of ducklings! ('Really?' I hear you ask...but time, it seems, is a great healer, or maybe we were just overcome with the luscious thought of duck dinners all year round).

On their first evening, the same thing happened as before, and two chicks were found pecking around in the bonfire ashes nearby, but from then on we had no further trouble. They even put themselves to bed, and it was lovely to see them running about enjoying the space, and indeed the sunshine, as the weather took a decided turn for the better... at last.

It soon became evident which of the youngsters were cockerels. With their upright gait and puffed out chests they would run up to each other, flare their neck feathers and eyeball one another, beak to beak. Sometimes this display would include a vertical jump into the air, just for good measure. It became very obvious that we had in fact nine hens and seven cockerels, and with a still increasing demand for eggs at the gate, we took the decision not to sell any of our hens after all.

Cordoning off the chick pen gave the teenagers plenty of space to play, safe from aerial attack and four-legged predators. The temporary netting that bisected the new chicken run to keep them contained, was weighted at the bottom with stones, and tied tightly at each end to the electric fence, preventing anyone from straying out of the protected area. However, before too long, it became evident that we again had a problem. One or two cockerels in the group seemed to repeatedly find themselves on the wrong side of the netting. Of course, once there, they also seemed totally incapable of finding their way back, and we were constantly occupied in tipping birds back over the netting. Try as we might, we couldn't ascertain *how* they got there; they were never actually caught in the act, they just appeared, and even to this day it remains a complete mystery to us.

Meanwhile, in the other run, the three Ms (Milly, Molly & Mandy) were starting to get a little braver, and were beginning to mingle tentatively on the edge of the group of older girls. Molly & Mandy were developing their combs and starting to look like fully grown-up chickens. Strangely, although supposedly the same age as the others, Milly still looked like a youngster, and there was little evidence of her comb as yet. I guessed that chickens must be similar to humans, in that we all develop at different rates.

The following morning, as I cleaned out the annexe, broom in hand and half a wary eye on Spence, I became aware of some shenanigans going on behind me. Turning around, I was met with the spectacle of Spence having his wicked way with Mandy. I glanced across to where her friends were standing. They were stood stock still, necks craned forward towards the action, and eyes unblinking in abject horror. As Spence climbed off her, Mandy ruffled her feathers, a little flustered, and her friends rushed forward to console her. Meanwhile Spence, the bounder, nonchalantly strutted away with a caddish air of inflated arrogance.

A couple of days later, I found our first egg from the three Ms tucked in the grass below the annexe. I guessed it might be Mandy's, and sure enough the next morning Mandy was found sitting in the 'granny annexe', laying what turned out to be the most extraordinarily long and eye-wateringly large egg for one so young.

A week or so later Molly was also producing eggs, though hers were soft-shelled to start with, and when she did produce a hard-shelled egg, it invariably had a dent in one end where it had obviously been launched from too great a height. I hoped she would perfect her technique soon, as eggs were in high demand.

10.   Trouble and Strife!

Our first summer saw a run of visitors, several trips across to England to see family and a wealth of local events to attend. There were food festivals, regattas, carnivals and agricultural shows. We also had the WIT (Women In Tune) festival practically on our doorstep.

Meanwhile, on the smallholding, our second lot of ducks were hatching. We were determined to learn by our mistakes and decided that August would surely be a drier month, circumventing many of the pitfalls we'd endured earlier in the year. All started well, as out of twelve eggs we achieved our best ever hatch of eleven, with just two ducklings needing a helping hand. Unfortunately though, one of the ducklings just wouldn't eat, and even with some force feeding, he sadly died three days later.

The others, however, went from strength to strength and at just two weeks of age, and with the weather much improved (in fact, positively balmy) we decided to move the ducklings outside. Initially I put them in a small pen on the lawn, which of course they did their best to decimate. I left them to it whilst I spread a layer of straw in the main duck run, which I hoped would deter the ducklings from creating a mud bath, as had been the case last time. This done, and as it was a hot day, I thought that they might like a short play on the pond; I could take my lunch down there and keep an eye on them, making a relaxing break for all of us.

To start with they loved it, some even diving below the water and resurfacing below the lily pads; all was going well and it was great fun watching them enjoying the water, as only ducks can. However, it was soon evident that their paddling feet were becoming more urgent and laboured. Some of the ducklings were also sitting ominously low in the water and plainly exhausted. Of course I was aware from previous experience that hand-reared ducklings are not waterproof, but I had seriously misjudged how long they would be buoyant for. I had also forgotten to allow for the fact that getting ten of them off the pond would be tricky, therefore prolonging the session still further. Unlike a mother duck, who can, with one quack, assemble her brood on the bank within seconds, I had no such authority, and the ducklings seemed oblivious to my efforts to urge them from the water.

I left Brian precariously balanced on the edge of the pond trying to grab passing ducklings, and ran to the garage for something we could use as a scoop. I scanned the garage for inspiration and arrived back at the pond with a grass rake and a hoe - not brilliant choices I know, but the best I could come up with in my panicked state. On my return I was relieved to see that the ducklings seemed to be managing by climbing onto the abundant lily pads and knots of pond weed, as well as hauling themselves into the reeds around the edge of the pond; they didn't seem to be in any imminent danger now, so I fetched a plank of wood and laid it as a ramp against the bank for them to climb out. With everything seemingly under control, Brian went off to get his lunch.

Of course they didn't use the plank - well that would have been just *too* easy - and unfortunately, I could now see that some of the ducklings were beginning to look quite distressed. I shouted to Brian for assistance and we tried to shepherd the ducklings into a corner using the hoe and a long garden cane, but they were sinking fast and we just could not get close enough with the grass rake to lift them out. Brian then spotted one duckling upside down, tangled in the reeds with its feet upper most. Without hesitation he valiantly launched himself into the water, shoes, socks, jeans and all! (I'd like to think he'd do the same for *me* if I was ever in a similar situation). He grabbed the sodden little body and passed it to me. The weight of it and the degree of sogginess suddenly made me realise that we had to get the others out rapidly; if we were not quick enough we could lose them all. I placed the rescued bird in the newly prepared run and returned to help Brian. He had reached another couple of strugglers in the reeds and was now knee deep, as the reeds he was stood on were beginning to give under his weight. We had no idea how deep the pond was, but that was not our immediate concern, we just had to reach all the birds as fast as possible. I counted the birds as they were rescued; we now had seven. There were three more to find. Brian had sight of two of them, but where was the third? Our eyes scanned the pond for a flash of yellow down, but we couldn't see any sign of the missing duckling. Maybe I had counted wrong, so I returned to the pen and counted again. No, there were definitely seven in the pen. Brian was just reaching the two he had spotted in the reeds as I returned to the edge of the pond. Then I looked down and saw the tail end of a little yellow body, right by my feet but very still. My heart pounded; what had I been thinking, putting them on the pond so young? I reached down to retrieve the sodden body. As I lifted it up it suddenly struggled; thankfully it was still alive, just utterly exhausted from trying to stay afloat. With all the ducklings now accounted for Brian emerged from the pond, water pouring from his canvas shoes and weighed down by his sodden jeans, but a true hero in mine, and ten other little pairs of eyes. Disaster had been averted. I couldn't believe we had come so close to losing every one of our ducklings.

In the duck run the victims of my stupidity were doing their best to dry out, and were diligently preening the pond weed from their down. They were definitely *not* up for exploring the little stream that trickled through the run (even though it was barely a couple of centimetres deep), and were instead just content to sit on the newly laid straw and recuperate after their traumatic experience.

Brian was also recovering, having stripped off on the patio and laid his clothes and shoes in the sun to dry, before showering off the duckweed and pungent sludge.

Calm was at last restored.

It was about now that we started to assess our successes and failures in the vegetable garden. Many others in the area had had a poor year with their veg, and it appeared that whatever we felt about our performance in the garden, we had done a lot better than most after such a wet season. We had enjoyed some great early potatoes, though our main potato crop had suffered problems with blight, resulting in a substantially reduced harvest. What's worse, the blight had then spread to our lovely tomato plants in the greenhouse, causing most of the plants to rot where they stood. Brian managed to save two or three plants, but had to burn the rest on the bonfire in an effort to halt the spread. Of course, Brian had also had his on-going battle with the dreaded slugs. Cauliflowers, cabbages and lettuces had all been totally decimated, despite the use of nematodes and 'helix tosta'. However, we had a good crop of runner beans (even though some slugs had managed to scale the eight foot canes and feast on a few of the beans). The peas did well too, and once past the early, vulnerable stage, they seemed pretty resistant to the slugs and the weather. Not that I saw many peas reaching the kitchen; certainly not enough to store away in the freezer for the winter. No, another fate lay in wait for the peas - Brian. Brian loves to pick them and eat them straight from the pod (as we all might, if only given half a chance). Indeed, when my parents were staying with us, Dad had taken me to one side and snitched that he had actually seen several peas surreptitiously pass Brian's lips whilst they had been in the veg patch together, and that, disappointingly, Brian had not thought to offer *him* a single one! The purple sprouting broccoli had done well; too well really, as it had reached maturity a good six months early, and then shot straight to seed. The beetroot were acceptable, but the carrots practically non-existent. However, the garlic, leeks, onions and shallots were all magnificent!

We gathered all the shallots - 8lb in all - and soaked them in brine overnight. Then the following day, we settled ourselves at the dining table and peeled them, our eyes smarting from the astringent vapour, and our hands stinging as the salty brine found its way into every cut and crevice. The shallots were then dropped into fresh brine and left for a couple of days, before they were bottled and topped up with pickling vinegar. It was good to get some stores put away, particularly after hearing how harsh the winters could be in the Cambrian Mountains, with snow rendering the roads impassable, often for weeks.

Being snowed-in though held no real fear for us, as long as we could gather plenty of supplies in the cold store and sacks of food and bedding for the animals. We'd have very little that needed doing outside, and aimed to spend the winter by the log burner planning what we'd grow the following year, the animals we'd raise and, no doubt, discussing our latest tactics for dealing with the surfeit of slugs!

As August drew to a close, the news broadcasters were declaring the summer as the wettest for 100 years, and still the rain came down, admittedly interspersed with some gloriously sunny days, which we certainly did not take for granted, as they had been so few and far between. Brian however, became very annoying with endless dismal asides about the weather... 'No post today? The postman's probably drowned.' It was bad enough having the grey, depressing weather, without the pessimism of your nearest and dearest, with whom you are stuck inside day after day as the rain is tossed against the windows by a howling gale. Even *my* optimistic heart was starting to accept that summer was just not going to happen this year.

To compound this dreariness, one of the young cockerels appeared to be going down with something. Perhaps he too, was fed up with the endless rain and was suffering from Seasonal Affective Disorder, as he stood apart from the others and closed his eyes. I decided to move him to the small run on the lawn, where he could sleep in peace and I could keep a better eye on him. At times like this my inexperience left me sadly lacking as a miracle worker, and all I could do was, once again, to try and glean some help from the internet. My biggest concern was that it might be coccidiosis, which apparently can affect young chickens, and being at a loss as to what to do, I thought I'd give him some chick crumbs to eat, which are medicated to help prevent coccidiosis. As it happened, having separated him from the others, it was clear that coccidiosis was probably not the problem, as he was not producing any yellowy liquid droppings. He was however, not eating a great deal, so something wasn't right, though what exactly was anybody's guess.

The following day he was no better, in fact as he bent to peck the ground he was actually sick, and with cold weather predicted, I made a small pen in the garage for him. On closer inspection I couldn't help but notice that his comb was distinctly bluish. The internet was now offering all sorts of scary scenarios for a blue comb, and it looked like the end of the road for my cockerel.

However, within a couple of days he was looking much perkier, though he didn't yet seem to have his appetite back. I tried to give him some company by moving my work to the garage. I was busy making a lamp from driftwood, which was a fiddly job, though quite therapeutic. I put Radio 4 on and worked quietly, sitting at a little table alongside his pen. Within minutes there was a little flutter and I had company on the arm of my chair. The cockerel seemed quite content to sit there, listening to 'Woman's Hour' and watching me work, and he fluffed out his feathers and settled comfortably at my side.

On the third day, the cockerel seemed a little bit better and I thought the company of his brothers might encourage him to eat properly again. I was also going to be out for most of the day and would not be able to indulge him in one of our affable bonding sessions, so I transferred him to the cockerel pen.

When I returned home later that afternoon, I was pleased to see my cockerel mixing with the others and finally eating normally again; another crisis had hopefully been averted.

In the top chicken coop Bossy Flossie was up to her old tricks, hogging the favourite nest box. Those who could cross their legs no longer, were forced to suffer her wrath in order to squeeze in next to her to deposit their eggs. There was of course another, perfectly serviceable nest box available right next to Flossie's, but that would have been far too simple, so most of the girls plumped for the riskier option, preferring to 'live life on the edge' a little. Why Flossie created such a fuss I can't imagine, as the others were actually providing eggs for *her* to sit on, which she'd eagerly and lovingly scoop under her as soon as they were laid. Of course *my* presence was met with an even greater degree of aggression, as she sat as wide as a dinner plate, swearing and trilling her warning as my hand searched beneath her underskirts for the precious eggs that she was doing her best to conceal.

Bossie Flossie's broodiness though could not be allowed to continue; I needed her back to laying duties as soon as possible. Egg production had already been seriously affected, with three soft-shelled eggs found in the 'granny annexe' that morning. I lifted her out of the cosy nest box and, ignoring her bad tempered protestations, plonked her in the wire cat basket which I'd propped up on bricks under the coop. With the breeze cooling her nether-regions for a few days, she would hopefully give up on her broodiness and return to duty.

Whatever crisis might be occurring on the smallholding, the geese could always raise my spirits. Squelching my way up to the chicken coop on the hill to collect the eggs one lunchtime, The Bully and his new best-friend and former victim, Titch, stood stock still under the drooping limbs of a small Buddleia bush. As I passed them only their eyes moved, tracking my course as they tried their best to be invisible (and failing that, to look the complete picture of innocence - both, it has to be said, lost causes).

With the geese now 'free-ranging' we tried to employ them gainfully in helping us to keep some of the rougher patches of grass down, where it was difficult to mow. The only problem with this was that it was really hard to keep the geese contained within the designated area, and understandably, they much preferred the lush green lawn near the house. However, as we didn't want to be dodging mounds of excrement every time we crossed the lawn, there was absolutely no room for negotiation and we stood firm.

On the part of the geese however, they were not prepared to rescind their 'right to roam', and their main mission each day was to make it to the lawn by whatever means they could. Watching the 'gang of four' hatch and execute their latest plan became a highly entertaining daily ritual, and we were regularly treated to cunningly clandestine and amusing antics of Oscar winning potential, suitably accompanied by the 'Mission Impossible' theme in the mists of our imaginations.

Between the geese and their target several overgrown patches of blackthorn and nettles formed natural barriers, as did the ditch with its equally overgrown banks. In between these natural obstacles we used whatever we could to plug the gaps, including wooden pallets, and even an extendable aluminium stepladder, hoping to thwart the invaders. However, with endless time to ruminate and a stubborn determination to achieve their objective, our geese were not ones to give up easily, and each day would see a new strategic assault on the forbidden lawn.

This latest attempt was obviously all about the ability to be invisible; an approach that still required some fine tuning, and perhaps the benefit of just a tad more natural cover than presently afforded by the young Buddleia. The reprobates were rounded up and once more returned to *their* side of the barrier, with a cacophony of chunterings and disgruntlement.

Of course the constant escape attempts were, at times, quite wearing, but the entertainment value far outweighed the hassle incurred. However, a few days after their failed attempt at invisibility, the geese went way too far, manifestly overstepping the line between amusement and tribulation, and outright war was declared. Our geese, it seemed, had morphed into delinquent teenagers overnight and were now totally running amok. Within minutes of being let out of their shed, they were in trouble. Brian, who had kindly offered to open the coop door for the chickens on the top field, found, on returning to the gate to connect the battery to the electric fence, that there was no longer a battery connector to connect; the geese had nibbled through the wire completely in the short time that he'd been in the run!

When I went down to muck-out the chickens, shortly after, I was in absolutely no mood for pleasantries. Being chased by 'The Bully' shaking his out-stretched beak at me in an increasingly threatening manner did little to assuage my irritation. I went about the business of filling feed containers and drinkers, tracking back and forth between the runs and the garage in seething silence, fully aware that my every move was being shadowed by 'the gang of four'. As I finished the coop on the bottom field and bent to reconnect the fence, I was greeted by yet more evidence of vandalism – those yobs had pulled the connector clean out of the side of the energiser and, just for good measure, had trampled it into the mud! With both the chicken fences now trashed, and not an ounce of remorse apparent, all 'free-ranging' was promptly suspended and the culprits unceremoniously banished to their run for the rest of the day. Meanwhile, repairs to the damaged wiring were undertaken, punctuated by mutterings of goose related obscenities.

11. Filling the freezers

After a fabulously warm and sunny week at the start of September, which we all appreciated, birds and humans alike, the weather turned a lot fresher as the month progressed and we willed the frosts to stay away, lest they bring an end to the bounty of beans we were busy harvesting and freezing.

We had already harvested the three short rows of beetroot, boiled them, skinned them and pickled them - one whole jar of them! It was disappointing I must say; I had hoped to have a good stock of beetroot on the shelves of the cold store. We would have to grow more next year.

However, the blackberries were ripening now, and there were plenty of large, juicy specimens to pick from the thickets around our fields. I tried putting a few small punnets on the stall and was surprised to find that they did actually sell, which amazed me, as there were plenty to pick along the hedgerows, and even right next to the stall! People, I supposed, were so short of time these days that even blackberrying was becoming a dying art - or could it be just good sense, to let someone else get torn to shreds by brambles, whilst you enjoy the fruit without the pain? My hands and legs were covered in scratches, which seemed to take a surprisingly long time to heal.

~

D-Day (Duck Day) loomed and preparations were made for the quick dispatch of our second batch of ducks. However, this time we were to have the help of our eldest son, Jack, and his girlfriend Ellie. Our last ducks had totally exhausted us, taking a good fourteen hours to dispatch, pluck, gut and bag, but this time we hoped for a much quicker and less stressful experience. Firstly, of course we had extra pairs of hands, but this time we hoped we had timed things better, and avoided the dreaded pin feathers that had taken so long to remove with tweezers. Also, Jack was keen to have another go at using his Whizbanger, which was a bit of a worry, as although it had indeed plucked one of the ducks last time, it had totally pulverised it in the process! However, we felt that if he could get the speed right, it would save us so much time and be well worth the effort.

Sadly, things did not go well. Brian had stipulated that the Whizbanger had just one chance; he was not prepared to risk the annihilation of any more of our hard earned duck meat. The first duck entered the Whizbanger, but it was soon evident that it was not going well. Again there were broken bones, though admittedly not as many as the first Whizbanger duck.

We resigned ourselves to doing it the hard way. Of course with four of us, the plucking was finished in half the time. After six hours, and with only a brief stop for coffee, all ten birds were plucked and laid out on the kitchen draining board ready for gutting and bagging. We had chosen to kill these ducks at seven weeks, slightly earlier than the previous batch, and although there were a few pin feathers, the timing was definitely better. However, the finished weight was disappointingly below that of our first ducks, by about 1lb per bird. This was surprising, as we had felt that with the first batch, they had not grown much in their eighth week, and had seemed to eat very little towards the end. The present batch however, had never really seemed to eat with the same gusto as the first, and we could only surmise that it was something to do with the difference in temperature and time of year.

With the ducks safely stored in the freezer, our focus was now on the geese, who had around four more weeks before it would be their turn. 'The Bully' had become noticeably more aggressive in recent weeks, and it was clear that keeping the geese over the winter and into the spring would only bring the territorial issues that most people associate with geese. This made the whole process of dispatching them just that little bit easier, as did the fact that they remained totally committed to creating as much mischief as they could before they went.

I made my way down to the younger chickens to clean them out, shadowed closely by the geese, 'The Bully' doing his now usual trick of snapping his beak in the direction of my rear end. As I entered the run and put my buckets down, 'The gang of four' watched from the open gate in the electric fence, contemplating their next move. Then, without warning, one of the gang trespassed into the chicken run, mistakenly thinking his mates were right behind him. The others though, had in fact thought better of the plan and turned tail, not wishing anyone to think they had anything to do with the misguided coup d'état. Of course, once aware that he was on his own, the intruder panicked, spreading alarm amongst the legitimate inhabitants, who ran about, well, like headless chickens! In the resulting melee, the lone goose lost all recollection of where the gate was and threw himself headfirst at the electric netting. Obviously with a very poor appreciation of his *actual* size, he seemed convinced of his ability to squeeze through one of the 10cm x 10cm squares in the netting, his weight and determination bending the fence posts double and bringing the netting flat to the ground. I quickly wrapped my arms around his huge bulk and pulled him backwards, but he was still intent on moving forwards, dragging us both into the fence. In desperation I grabbed his neck and, with some resistance, I finally persuaded him through the open gate to join his mates, who were now grazing a safe distance away, denying ever having met the 'numpty' who had just been ejected in their direction.

~

As the first frosts of early October tickled the vegetation and the landscape became peppered with gold and bronze, it was clear that autumn was on its way. Much to Brian's great delight we were still harvesting an abundance of runner beans, and being one of the few gardeners in the district to have had such success in the face of the widely acknowledged dire growing season, he was justifiably proud of his achievement. We now had over forty portions of beans in the freezer and were beginning to cast around for other ways to store our glut. Runner bean chutney, it seemed, would fit the bill, and whilst searching for a recipe, I also stumbled across one for Bramble Chutney. As we still had quite a few blackberries in the fields, I decided that was worth a try too.

~

With the reduction of daylight hours, together with the autumn moult, egg production was now declining significantly and we were down to just three or four eggs from our eight laying hens. Meanwhile, the young chickens that we'd bred were maturing nicely. One of the cockerels was even beginning to develop his crow, and at first light he could be heard attempting to match his father's 'Cock-a-doodle dos' emanating from the coop on the hill. The youngster's efforts however, sounded more like a cuckoo with a sore throat than a virile young cockerel...but it was a start.

This exhibition of course, only served to remind us that the cockerels would soon need to be moved to what was rapidly becoming known as 'Death Row' (aka 'The Duck Run'). Here they could be fed a poultry finisher mix for the last four weeks, as opposed to the layers pellets that the young hens were now enjoying. A tinge of sadness pricked my conscience, as I marvelled at the beautiful gold and auburn feathers of the cockerels; some of them would make magnificent adult specimens, given the opportunity. However, I needed to be strong; keeping seven cockerels on a smallholding of just three acres would be, quite frankly, asking for trouble! Spence had already shown us the strife we could be burdening ourselves with - even 'one' cockerel could be too many! I did consider trying to sell some of the cockerels, but everyone I asked seemed knee deep in cockerels as it was. So 'Death Row' it would be, and I consoled myself with the knowledge that they had enjoyed a wonderful quality of life whilst they'd been at Nantcoed.

Meanwhile, the geese were not growing as fast as we had hoped. They had recently been allowed to venture onto the lush lawn (as we were now spending more time indoors) and had been treated to poultry finisher for the last three weeks, so we expected to see a significant difference in their bulk and weight. But geese, it seems, are resistant to any change in their routine.

Previously, they had relished their bedtime feed of layers pellets, and indeed could hardly wait! Evening after evening, they would clumsily step over the now pretty inadequate array of obstacles which had previously kept them off the patio, and make a bee-line for the patio doors, where they would constantly tap their beaks on the glass and peer at us, heads cocked to one side then the other, eight beady eyes enquiring as to whether we'd forgotten that they hadn't had their supper yet. Each day the pestering got earlier and earlier, until their badgering routine was kicking-off half way through the afternoon!

Although the poultry finisher was apparently not as appetising, the pestering continued and we felt compelled to come up with a solution. So we decided to restrict the geese to their run, where the grass was short and well nibbled. Without a great deal of grass they would surely be keen to eat the finisher pellets, which we made sure were freely available all day. The biggest bonus of course, was that they could no longer get to the patio and we could once again enjoy sitting in the lounge, unmolested by drumming beaks and expectant faces at the window.

With the geese below their target weight at the 24 week deadline we'd originally set for their dispatch, we were forced to have a rethink. In order to avoid the dreaded pin feathers, we really needed to do them by 26 weeks at the latest, and so the geese became subjected to repeated and hopeful squeezes and prods over the following few days, in an effort to determine any increase in plumpness.

However, at 26 weeks we had yet another hectic weekend of visitors, and so the geese continued to ride their luck. In fact even when our visitors had gone, we had a series of events that still prevented us from getting on with processing the geese. It was actually almost a week later that we finally did the deed.

Regardless of my reservations about having the geese in the first place, and my recurring annoyance at the delinquent behaviour of 'the gang of four' in more recent months, it was really quite sad to see the geese meet their end. They had been great 'lawn mowers' and it seemed a tad ungrateful to finish them off. But their time had come and we did everything we could to make it as stress-free and as quick as possible.

Plucking a goose, we knew, would be a big job, and we decided that it would be best to work together on one bird at a time, so that we could complete the plucking whilst the bird was still reasonably warm, making the job much easier. As it was, each bird took us about an hour to pluck, starting with the wings, then the legs and back, and finally the breast. A goose though, has an incredible number of feathers and within a very short time goose-down hung in the air like snowflakes, gathering on every surface and object in the garage. Fine filaments tickled our nostrils and clung to our eyebrows and eyelashes. The fine down covered us from head to toe, and even attached itself to the stubble on Brian's face, which, combined with his now white, feather trimmed woolly hat, gave him an uncanny resemblance to Father Christmas!

Four, we decided, was more than enough to pluck in a day, and a mental note was made not to exceed this number, if we did geese again. Our fingers and thumbs were sore and our backs ached by the time we had finished. After a brief break for a sandwich and a cup of tea, we re-grouped for the gutting, weighing and bagging process. Although the geese appeared to vary quite a bit in size, the dressed weight of each bird was pretty similar, the smallest being 11lb and the other three coming out at 12lb 3oz. As predicted by all the books we'd read, the smaller youngsters did gain weight and catch the larger birds up by the end. 'The Bully', who had been first to hatch, and for the whole summer had been definitely the biggest bird (and most aggressive), actually came out at the same weight as 'the twins', and not really that much bigger than 'Titch'.

Looking at the prices of geese on-line (organic of course), we would probably have had to pay £60 - £65 per bird, so we felt well satisfied to have produced our birds for no more than £10 each. We would definitely have geese again, we decided!

12. Things that go bump!

George and Oliver, the two Shetland ponies that had spent the summer nibbling away at the shockingly poor pasture on the lower field, had done an excellent job of bringing the long grass and reeds under control. The large bramble patches however, remained untouched, havens for a handful of rabbits, and more worryingly, likely cover for foxes. We considered the possibility of getting a couple of pigs, who would hopefully put pay to the more stubborn tussocks, and the brambles too with luck, but in the meantime the ponies were moved onto the slopes of the top field to work their magic on the overgrown pasture there.

With the ponies safely out of the way, we decided to fell a large Silver Birch tree, that stood next to the ditch running between the two fields. It cast quite a substantial shadow over our chickens on the top field in the morning, and over the young chickens on the bottom field in the afternoon. When in full leaf, it also blocked our view of the village from the chalet. This tree though, was far too big for us to fell on our own. Soon after we'd arrived at Nantcoed, Brian had taken a dislike to a much smaller Silver Birch, which stood on the top field at the edge of the veg patch, and which he accused of taking far too much light from his plants in the greenhouse. The tree, though tall, was no more than a thin whip of a tree with no real breadth to its trunk, so we lassoed it with a rope, which I was instructed to keep taut so as to ensure the tree fell into the field, and not onto the greenhouse. As Brian's handsaw chewed through the last few centimetres of trunk however, it became shockingly and rather belatedly clear to me that the greenhouse was in grave danger, as even the whole and not insignificant weight of my body appeared totally ineffectual in counterbalancing that of the tree. It was only by sheer good luck that it missed the greenhouse altogether on its wayward descent.

The large Silver Birch, whose trunk was a good 60cm in diameter, was a much heftier proposition and we sensibly enlisted the help of a knowledgeable friend who had felled many trees in his time, and came with his own chainsaw. The area was assessed and there seemed to be enough room for the tree to simply fall across the ditch and into the lower field. The run where the young chickens were housed was close by, but at what appeared to be a safe distance away. However, I shepherded the chickens to the furthest end of their run and put some netting across to keep them there, just to be on the safe side.

The chainsaw roared into action, and in no time at all an almighty crack could be heard as the tree tottered, and then fell with an impressive crr...ashhh! It was good to see it landing pretty well where we had hoped it would land. However, whether it was the resulting down-draught, or just an injection of mass hysteria prompted by a tree falling from the sky, I don't know, but as the tree went down, every one of the young chickens simultaneously shot up into the air and over the far end of their fence! To add to the chaos, despite the tree falling away from, and absolutely nowhere near the other chicken run on the hill behind us, Spence and two of the Ms decided to catapult themselves over *their* fence too.

With the evening drawing in and the light quickly fading, all hands were employed in returning everyone to the safety of their respective runs; a task confounded by the fragility of the escapees frayed nerves. Frantic silhouettes flitted back and forth in pursuit of eleven traumatised chickens, and one brave soul waved a large landing net in the direction of a rather vocal and extremely irate cockerel.

~

As we moved into November, the weather incredibly remained very wet, interspersed with brief but heavy hail storms, and rivulets of water carved channels down the top field. It was becoming noticeably chillier, and the frosts had now completely put pay to the runner beans and raspberries in the garden. Cleaning out the chickens each morning became a chore, especially when the temperature was well below zero. The young cockerels however, continued as ever to provide some light relief as Spence, giving his very best 'Cock-a-doodle-doo' from the coop on the hill behind me, was answered by an earnest but less sophisticated 'Cuck-doo-a' from the far side of the lower field. These comical impersonations of their father kept me chuckling, despite the cold nipping at my fingers.

The cockerels now had just two more weeks left and unfortunately they were beginning to show some of their Dad's worst traits. They would peck at my knees and wellies when I entered the pen, and even flare their neck feathers and posture threateningly. Although I had thus far managed to tough it out, by just picking them up and moving them out of the way, I felt quite vulnerable when I was crouched down cleaning out their hut, particularly when three or four of them were perched on the roof immediately above my head. I had had enough encounters with Spence to know how quick and dangerous their beaks and claws could be, not to mention unpredictable. I just hoped we could last the next couple of weeks on reasonably affable terms.

Just a few days later however, it was clear that one cockerel in particular was going to be trouble. As soon as he heard me sliding the bolts on the gate back, he was there posturing, with shoulders held out as broad as his frame would allow and the feathers on his neck splayed in threat. He then made every attempt to lunge his pointy beak in the direction of various body parts. Cockerels appeared adept at finding the tiniest piece of exposed skin, and this one scored a direct hit to my knee through a rip in my jeans. I was at my most susceptible of course, when cleaning out their hut. On doing so, it had seemed a good idea, to eject all the cockerels from the hut before I started, so as to avoid anyone pecking me in the eye, but this then put my rear end at a distinct disadvantage. bent double, and with my midriff exposed as I stretched in on all fours, several vindictive lunges were endured by my nether regions, and the pain at times made me squeal quite loudly. Goodness knows what anyone walking past on the lane might have imagined was going on!

A week later, the aggression in the cockerel pen had stepped up a notch; not in my direction this time, but towards one of their own. When I entered the pen to clean them out and top up their feeder, one cockerel was squeezed down the side of the hut, looking very sorry for himself and with his back to the rest of them. On closer inspection there was also some blood on the grass in front of him. I lifted him onto the roof of the hut and went about my duties. All seemed to be fine and I hoped it was just a one-off skirmish, but I kept an eye on him all the same.

However, very soon there was further trouble; this time several birds were joining in, so I quickly extracted him from the fracas. Unable to stay where he was, I now had to find somewhere I could put this cockerel. There was only one option really, so I popped him into a cordoned off section of the run where I had young hens. I sorted out some food and water for him and Brain and I manoeuvred the goose shelter down the hill on the wheelbarrow for him, so that he would be able to get out of the gusts of wind blowing up the field from the valley below. Not that our cockerel seemed to appreciate the lengths we had gone to to make him comfortable. No, he was much more concerned with parading himself along the fence dividing him from the girls. The girls on the other side were equally enamoured by their new neighbour, and scrambled to get as close as they could to this virile young man, as he gave them his best 'cock-er-dooo' and strutted back and forth. Everywhere our cockerel went, he was shadowed by a wanton crowd of adoring young hens, mirroring his every move and unable to take their eyes off him. I went off to do a few jobs, now that all seemed well in the chicken runs.

When I returned an hour later, to check on our cockerel, he was not where I had left him. It didn't take long though, to work out that our cockerel had scaled the fence and landed himself amidst his besotted fans. There he stood, looking very pleased with himself, surrounded by a mass of dizzy headed girls, admiration oozing from every feather. I returned him to his side of the fence, much to the disgust of the girls, where he seemed content to recover from the stresses and strains of being adored - for a little while anyway.

~

With winter approaching fast, we were pleased to have our new woodburner that would run our central heating. In an effort to save money in the future, we hoped to be able to run the heating on wood alone; wood that we had managed to accrue for free over the past few months, whilst carrying out some much needed maintenance on our overgrown boundaries. The system though, could still be run on oil if needed, or even a mixture of the two, with one boosting the other. It would also heat our hot water. The old boiler, originally designed for solid fuel, had been converted to oil by the previous owner. The outcome was the noisiest boiler you could imagine, and any visitors had to be pre-warned of its roar, so as to avoid undue alarm as it fired into action.

Getting the new system installed had not been easy. Just getting a plumber to look at the job had been frustratingly difficult. We had eventually managed to contact four plumbers who agreed to look at the job. The first two came, looked, promised to send a quote, and then disappeared never to be seen again. The third was the husband of a friend, who was honest enough to tell us that the job was too big for him, and the fourth actually seemed to be the man for the job. He was the only one who looked in the attic, checked the whole system and gave us a referee to ring, who was someone he'd done a similar job for. And he actually *did* send a quote. Of course each person had a different idea as to how to complete the work, some wanting to take up floorboards and fit various pumping systems in inconvenient places, such as the corner of the dining room!

Originally we had thought to use the new woodburner to heat just the downstairs rooms; particularly 'the library' at the north end of the house, which was cold and musty. Having had a fabulous Clearview woodburner in our last place, Brian was convinced this was the answer and we found a great shop selling just what we wanted in a nearby town. We managed to do a deal on an ex-display model and had it delivered, not realising it would take another six weeks or so to find a plumber to install it! However, it turned out that our best option was to heat the whole house, and the water, in tandem with the oil, and therefore we had bought the wrong model for the job. We then had to persuade the shop to exchange the Clearview for a different model. They were surprisingly accommodating in actual fact and a deal was soon done. The job, it transpired, was going to be a lot more expensive than we had originally budgeted for. We hoped though, that in the long run it would be the right choice, and the most cost effective option. I must admit it was quite scary to see such a chunk taken out of our slowly diminishing funds.

When the plumber eventually arrived to do the job, which we had been informed would take around four days to complete, it was clear that early morning starts were not his thing, and he and his assistant arrived most mornings at around 10.30am/11am and often left by 3pm, sometimes earlier. The job in fact took eight days, during which the plumbers traipsed wet muddy boots in and out of the house constantly, managing every time to find that one spot that was not covered by the dust sheets that I'd carefully laid over the lounge rug and the oak flooring, in a vain attempt to preserve the floors.

Having arrived on the Monday, by Friday we had the woodburner in situ, with two sturdy copper pipes projecting from it, up the wall and through two neatly cut holes in the ceiling. The thermal store tank was positioned in the loft above the lounge and connected by an incredible quantity of pipes. Before leaving, the plumbers gave instructions as to a possible course of action, should anything start to leak in their absence, and we were assured that we still had hot water available to us over the weekend by way of the old immersion heater, which they had reconnected. As we had been without hot water for two days and we were planning on going out that night to a quiz night in the village hall, we were looking forward to a shower. However, the immersion was incredibly slow and after being on for two hours the water was barely tepid. We abandoned hope of a shower, switched off the immersion and went out, hoping that we didn't smell too unsavoury. We would try again in the morning, when we had more time to wait for the immersion to do its stuff.

'I can hear water!' came the call the next morning from the bottom of the stairs, just seconds after Brian had brought me my cup of tea. I leapt out of bed, not delaying to put on a dressing gown, and flew down the stairs.

'Get a towel,' I shouted, as I reached behind the lobby door for the pole with which to open the hatch above the lounge. Swinging the hatch door open and pulling the ladder down as quickly as I could, I ascended into the loft space to be met with water spraying across the planked joists at an alarming rate. It appeared to be coming from one of the soldered joints in the new piping.

'Grab me another towel!' I barked at Brian.

There was already quite a puddle forming beneath the pipe, which threatened to ruin the beautiful oak ceiling below. I quickly wrapped the towel around the joint in the pipe and squeezed hard, to little affect. With my other hand I bent down and turned the two red stopcocks clockwise, hoping that these would stem the flow. I stood gripping the towel tight, trying to think what else we could do.

'Turn the water off in the garage,' I bellowed to Brian below in the lounge.

I heard him open the back door, but before I heard the sound of the garage door opening it was clear that the flow from the pipe was starting to diminish at last. We breathed a sigh of relief, and whilst Brian rang the plumber I went back to bed to drink my now lukewarm tea, and allow my palpitations to subside.

The plumber eventually turned up to mend the joint several hours later, with his usual lack of haste. Before he left, he sagely grinned and recounted the difficulties we could be in for if there were similar leaks when he returned on Monday to fire up the woodburner for the first time. With the water under added pressure, he warned, the results could be spectacular and on a whole new level! It didn't do anything to make our weekend any more restful, and I made a mental note to have a stack of old towels ready to hand when the plumbers returned.

As it happened, the firing up of the woodburner went well and our worries about the dreaded leaks turned out to be unjustified. We had hot water and the radiators were warm. The plumber agreed to return on Wednesday, to carry out any tweaking that was needed, but otherwise the job was done.

~

What is it with cockerels? They seem to live from one minor crisis to the next; our Spence certainly did! How he did it I have no idea, but he had managed to cut his foot twice in the space of a few weeks, and by doing nothing more than sitting on his perch overnight! The girls hadn't had any such problem; goodness knows what he was getting up to in 'the wee small hours'. The signs were evident as soon as I opened the coop; a patch of bright red, bloodied sawdust just inside the door. Everyone piled out as normal, but it wasn't difficult to see who had the problem. Spence stood on one leg over by the fence, looking distinctly sheepish, most definitely not his usual self. When he did move, it was with huge, exaggerated steps, lifting his left leg higher and stretching it forward longer than was strictly necessary. It made for quite a comical scene, in a John Cleese, 'Ministry of Silly Walks' sort of way, and if I hadn't have been so worried that we may be in for an expensive trip to the vet, I'm sure I could have more fully appreciated the humour of it all.

Not wishing to aggravate the injury, I decided against trying to catch him in what had become the only way possible - with the landing net - but opted to see how things went. The following day though, there was more bloodied sawdust, and it was evident that poor Spence was not even feeling up to his usual game of 'chase' with the girls; things must have been bad! It looked as though I would have to catch him after all.

However, by the time I had cleaned the coops out and had my breakfast, Spence seemed to be moving much more easily, and as the rain was now lashing the hillside, and the ground sodden and slippery, I decided conditions were far too treacherous for any kind of attempt at capture.

The following morning dawned crisp and sunny though, and the mist lingered in the valley below us. If Spence was no better, I decided, I really would have to try and catch him. He stood on a small tussock, with his left leg tucked under him, his gaze fixed on the valley and his upright stance endeavouring to convey an illusion of authority. I bravely eased myself towards him, one foot at a time and crouched dangerously low. His left eye fixed me and I prudently plotted my best escape route. Thankfully though, he stayed put. As I got within a metre, he dropped his left foot a little and at last I got a clear view of the problem. He appeared to have a small cut, no longer than 1cm, on one side of his foot, similar to a paper cut. It looked as though it would probably heal on its own, though if he had been easier to catch I might have dipped it in some salty water for him, to help the healing process. As it was, I withdrew to a safe distance and left him to it. Just a few hours later, quite obviously on the mend, he was spotted 'surprising' several of the girls. The old Spence was evidently back!

Unbelievably, November saw a still worse turn in the weather, which few thought possible after the summer we'd had. Lashing rain and 75mph winds whipped the valley, as well as much of the UK, for several days. By the end of the third day, the chicken run on the hill looked more like a waterfall as the ground could absorb no more, and cascades issued from every crevice. Not that it made much difference to the chickens, as they rarely ventured from the coop; those that did, risked losing what few feathers they still had left, being several weeks into their annual moult, and excursions were sensibly kept to an absolute minimum. Chickens and cockerels sat hunched and thoroughly fed-up in every coop. We humans felt much the same, and tried to make the most of the enforced respite from the outdoor chores. The wind tore at the roof and stone walls. The windows hissed and the doors rattled as the storm raged outside, and we prayed that we'd get through the storm unscathed.

As darkness began to fall, I donned my raincoat, pulled on my wellies, and announced that I was going to put the chickens to bed. Pulling up my hood and grasping it tight around my chin, I launched myself into the deluge. The wind whipped at my face as I picked my way through the mud to the coop on the upper field. As I arrived at the electric fence, it was clear there was a problem, as loud cracks of electricity shorted from a stretch further up the hill. I struggled up the bank to where the problem seemed to be. The fence, it appeared, was sitting in a good ten centimetres of water. The wind wrenched the hood from my hand and rain seeped down the back of my neck, as I battled my way back to the garage to fetch a spade. I attempted to release the water by digging channels down the hillside away from the fence. Although not perfect, the plan seemed to alleviate the worst of the shorting, and the fence could be reconnected. By now it was completely dark and I turned my attention to the young chickens on the lower field. Water was streaming through their run too, but it didn't seem to be interfering with the electric fence, thankfully. However, part of the fence had been beaten almost flat by the force of the wind and I had to stake it. By the time I returned to the house some 45 minutes later, I was completely soaked to the skin and chilled to the core.

I stood in the doorway of the dining room, dripping from head to foot, puddles forming around my feet and my hair wildly askew, concerned that Brian might have been worrying about what had become of me, and ready to allay his fears and console him.

Was he 'heck as like'!

Brian was, in fact, bent double over his jigsaw puzzle on the dining table, warming his backside on the woodburner that roared behind him, completely and utterly oblivious to my demise.

'Didn't you wonder where I was?' I asked, water dripping from my hood and trickling down my frozen cheeks.

'No,' he said, not even lifting his head to look in my direction, 'I just thought you were talking to the chickens.'

'Talking to the chickens? What? In the pouring rain and gale force winds? In the dark?'

It was a good job I hadn't succumbed to the atrocious conditions, slipped or twisted my ankle, broken any bones or needed rescuing; hypothermia would surely have been an absolute certainty, death presumably claiming me long before I'd even been missed!

Later that night, I was once again fighting the elements - this time though, I made sure Brian was with me and getting just as soggy. Returning from taking Storm for his last walk before bedtime, Brian checked on the stream. The water gushed down the field above us and along the far side of the bank that bordered our drive, until it took a swerve right, dipping under the drive by the gate and continuing along the boundary between the lower field and the lane, in the process passing just feet from our front door. Something seemed to be causing the water to back up and the stream looked close to bursting its banks. It didn't take us too long to spot a large plastic storage box that must have been tossed into the stream by the wind earlier in the day, but we couldn't reach it without risking slipping down the bank and into the raging torrent that now swept past the house. The blackness of the night and the persistent lashing rain hindered our efforts still further. Fetching the broom from the patio I quickly handed it to Brian, whilst I held the torch for him. He pushed the broom into the water and after several misses eventually managed to hook the box out onto the bank. We then used the broom to push the knots of twigs and leaves that had gathered in the reeds at various points along the stream, forming small but effective dams. At last the water started to escape, tumbling down the hill and away from the house.

The following day saw a brief respite from the storms, and we used it wisely, removing anything that might cause further blockages in the stream and digging out debris from the ditches near to the house, in order to allow the water free passage away from the property. Chatting to the postman that morning, it appeared that we'd been luckier than many, with several trees blocking roads on the mountain and both roads into town from the village blocked by flood water. Several cars apparently lay abandoned in hedges.

Each wave of storms that hit us over the following week, was interspersed with severe overnight frosts, and the wintry conditions seemed to spur the fox into bolder sorties than normal. One morning, just as I was getting dressed, there came a shout from Brian downstairs. A large dog fox had just strolled nonchalantly across the patio! I raced to the bedroom window, and flung it wide as the fox arrogantly strolled towards the run where our young cockerels stood innocently unaware of the impending danger. I threw my buxom figure across the wide windowsill and leaned out into the chill air, dressed only in my bra and knickers and bellowed piercing obscenities like some bawdy wench. The fox stopped dead, his head slowly turning to glance over his shoulder. Startled by my near naked body dangling from the upstairs window, he spun around instantly and bolted down the field, through the fence and out onto the lane.

Much to Brian's immense amusement, it was months before the fox plucked up the courage to attempt a foray onto our land again.

~

A few days after their close call with the fox, our cockerels had a date with the freezer. Sad as it was to see them go, it would be good to have one less coop to clean out over the winter, and I certainly wouldn't miss the sharp jabs from their beaks.

We decided to give the 'Whizbanger' one final chance to redeem itself; after all it *was* really designed to pluck chickens, not ducks. This time, with a little tweaking to the speed of the motor, the birds tumbled around splendidly, just as they should. I aimed the hose into the barrel to wash off the feathers, and as I stopped the machine, it was clear that it was an unprecedented success! Each bird took less than a minute to pluck, and within two hours we had dispatched and plucked all six cockerels, tidied up the mess and were sat with our feet up drinking coffee! It was unheard of...dispatching days usually resulted in a good seven hours of hard work, sore fingers and thumbs and being too exhausted to cook the dinner. We were delighted and rang Jack to let him know that all his hard work hadn't been in vain after all, and that the 'Whizbanger' *did* work with chickens.

The cockerels all came out at around 4lb 10oz, which was only about half a pound less than the last lot of ducks we'd done. The problems with the Whizbanger obviously weren't due to the *weight* of the birds. The only thing we could think of was that it was due to the *shape* of the bird. The longer, more angular duck, presumably, was less likely to roll around the barrel of the 'Whizbanger', whereas a chicken is a much rounder bird. Whatever the rationale, we ended the year on a glorious high.

13.   Too close for comfort

With less to do on the smallholding now that the harvest was gathered and stored, it was time to get organised for Christmas. Presents were purchased and wrapped, mince pies baked and frozen and cards written. All was pretty much sorted a good two weeks before the big day...which was lucky as it turned out.

The big Silver Birch that we had felled a few weeks earlier, had lain untouched on the field as other chores, and the inclement weather, had demanded our attention. Brian was, however, keen to get the logs cut and stacked so that they could season properly. Leaving them on the wet ground would only cause them to rot, and we hated to see good firewood wasted.

Brian took his saw-horse and chainsaw down the field to where we would be working. I quickly tidied up the garage, ready for our youngest's return from uni at the end of the week; he had a lot of work to do on his car whilst he was home, and wouldn't appreciate having to climb over bales of straw and bags of layers pellets to reach his tools. This done, I made my way down the field to help Brian.

He had sorted out some small stuff that needed chopping up before we tackled the main trunk.   It was a bitterly cold morning and I was glad that I'd thought to wrap up warm with several layers of clothing, including a pair of thermal long-johns that I'd bought for Brian years ago, but which he'd never fancied wearing.

I was used to holding the logs on the saw-horse for Brian to cut, but these smaller branches were fiddly; despite me wrestling with them they just wouldn't sit straight. We had only cut a couple of these unruly branches when the chainsaw suddenly jumped, clipping my gloved hand. At first the enormity of what had just happened didn't register, but as I removed my glove to survey the damage it was clear that more than an Elastoplast would be required.

Not wanting to alarm Brian, who despite being able to deftly dispatch ducks and chickens is strangely squeamish when it comes to human blood and gore, I shielded the wound from him and headed back to the house to rinse it under the tap. As I leant over the sink though, it was immediately obvious that this was going to involve a trip to the hospital, and as we were at least 50 minutes from the nearest hospital I needed to move fast. I was losing a lot of blood, and more worryingly, there appeared to be parts of my hand flapping about that I'd never seen before, such as tendons and nerves. Brian searched for something to wrap my hand in whilst I tried to wash as much debris out as I could.

It was at this point that there came a knock on the door and a cheery 'Hello'; I had forgotten that I had invited Chloe, a friend from the village, for coffee, and she now appeared like a guardian angel to the rescue. Brian soon wiped the smile off her face by telling her that he had cut my hand and I was in the bathroom. She, presuming he just meant I'd cut it with a knife in the kitchen, came through to the bathroom to survey the damage. Totally unprepared for what she saw, the air was briefly filled with an avalanche of expletives, until I quietly persuaded her to tone her comments down so as not to worry Brian any more than he already was. Once over her initial shock, Chloe was brilliant and instantly morphed into 'responsible adult mode'. Before long my hand was wrapped up tight in a bandage and a tea-towel and, with Brian left to take care of the smallholding in our absence, we were in her car heading south for the hospital.

Once at the A & E department in Carmarthen, and having been deposited in a warm side room to be assessed, I was now regretting the layers of clothing I had cocooned myself in that morning. As they sort to lower my temperature and peel back my embarrassingly tatty work-clothes, it was only a matter of time before my mortification was complete, and the doctor's stethoscope reached the long-johns.

Not content with revealing my bizarre underwear to the staff of one hospital, I was soon transferred and winging my way to a whole new and unsuspecting group of hospital staff. With the initial assessment attained, numbed by injections and dosed with painkillers, I was back in the car and heading for the specialist plastic surgeons in Swansea. Having had nothing to eat or drink since breakfast, not even that coffee Chloe had come round for, we were by now both feeling distinctly lightheaded. The staff at Moriston Hospital in Swansea were lovely though, and as soon as it was established that I would be having a local anaesthetic for my operation and not a general, we were both brought hot cups of tea and sandwiches. It was now around 5pm, and I urged Chloe to ring Brian to give him an update on what was happening, knowing that he would be beside himself with worry.

By 6pm I was in the operating theatre prepped for my op. It went well, and despite being told I would probably need a skin graft from my thigh to cover my knuckle, the surgeon worked his magic and the graft thankfully wasn't needed after all. In fact I was lucky all round, having missed actually cutting through any of the tendons or nerves, and only having chipped a small piece off my knuckle bone. I was stitched back together and given a wide half plaster cast with my fingers bent almost at right angles. I returned to the ward, where we waited for another hour and a half for my tetanus jab and some antibiotics. By the time we finally returned home it was 10.15pm and we were all exhausted, not least Brian, who had understandably fretted for the last eleven hours about the possible extent of my injuries, coming up with increasingly dire scenarios as the day had progressed, so that by the time we returned home he looked almost as rough as I did!

The day had been a lesson for us all. Accidents can happen to any of us, at any time, and although we had always treated the chainsaw with respect and been very careful, it was clear we should have thought to invest in some specialist protective clothing. Chloe and I had also learnt that it is a good idea to know where the nearest A&E department is, and better still to know how to get into the car park in an emergency; we had frustratingly found it necessary to perform a couple of drive-bys on our arrival, before we chanced upon the entrance. We also concluded that keeping a list of your neighbours' phone numbers with you at all times and not just on your mobile (mobiles tending to go flat just as you need them most) was a good idea, just in case you need to ask someone to feed and walk your dogs, should you unexpectedly find yourself needing to take a friend to the hospital. It is also a good idea to have an extra key cut and leave it with a friend in the village, so they can actually get *in* to feed and walk your dogs. Other lessons learnt were: keep a spare Twix in your bag in case your injured friend is 'nil by mouth' and you are hungry (if she is told she is having a local anaesthetic, you can easily share half with her should you be feeling generous). Avoid unusual underwear if there is the slightest chance that a trip to hospital is on the books - no matter how cold it is. Before leaving for the hospital pick up your glasses, so that you will be able to read the mountain of forms they will ask you to sign whilst you're there, and at *all* costs, and however bad you feel, keep your sense of humour when using the toilet in the specialist hand injury ward, as above the sink it insensitively asks you to, 'Please use two hands when pulling the paper towel from the dispenser'.

On my return from hospital, Brian was endearingly diligent in attending to my every need, making me a cup of tea and a cheese sandwich, and ensuring I was as warm and comfortable as possible. Unfortunately, 24 hours later this was but a distant dream, as he tried to juggle his normal chores with the added burden of doing the chickens and helping me to get dressed.

To add to his troubles the weather took another dip, and torrential rain drenched him as he went about his extra chores, and, to add to his woes still further, the young chickens impishly seemed intent on taking full advantage of the situation. With half their run cordoned off to give it a chance to recover from the ravages of eighteen scratching feet, the youngsters were having great fun squeezing through a gap beneath their coop into the forbidden area, so Brian found himself constantly engaged in either coaxing them back under the netting, or running to and fro in an effort to apprehend the offenders and deposit them back over the fence.

The youngsters also seemed compelled to oversee the quality of Brian's work as he cleaned out their coop each morning, and insisted on standing in groups just where he was trying to clean. Being so tame and naturally inquisitive, the girls would not be persuaded to wait outside, or even to move slightly to one side, and so 'doing the chickens', which I could normally do in half an hour, was slowly developing into a whole morning's work.

The egg laying rate also fell - leading me to believe that my girls were not being treated to the gentle, reassuring chats that they were generally used to. Judging by the increasingly disgruntled mutterings issuing from Brian's lips as he tracked his way back up the field from the chicken coops each morning, 'cosy chats' were probably not top of the list.

In an effort to offer some assistance and ease the load a little, I thought I'd attempt to clean the eggs before they were boxed up and put out on the stall. This I normally did with a piece of fine sandpaper, a simple job with two hands, but a pretty tricky manoeuvre with just one. I rested the egg in a towel and did my best to hold it still with my plastered hand, whilst I rubbed the egg with the sandpaper with my right hand. Sometimes, although a slow process, it worked, but all too often I misjudged the pressure that my plastered hand was exerting, and I was left with an eggy mess. It was soon decided that my 'help' was the sort that created *more* work, not less, and I was promptly relieved of my duties.

The ponies too, seemed to know that Brian was under increased pressure, and chose the one morning that he was alone on the smallholding, to run amok. Chloe, had kindly offered to take me down to Sam's uni in Swansea to fetch him home for the holidays (me of course, being unable to drive). Having escaped from their cordoned off end of the field, George and Oliver were having a whale of a time, running across the lawn leaving deep hoof-shaped pits in the wet ground, and chasing round and round the chicken runs, knocking out the guy ropes that held the electric fences up. Meanwhile, Brian hastily tried to find the phone number for their owners, him not being a 'horsey person' in any way, shape or form. Brian likes his horses at a safe distance, and preferably with a strong fence in between. This aside, no matter how horsey or expert one might be, this was obviously a job for more than one person, as the two pranksters did not look anywhere near ready for 'throwing in the towel'. Enjoying every bit of mischief they were creating with their new-found freedom, adrenalin coursed through their veins, making them surprisingly nippy on their feet.

Even with the arrival of the ponies' owners, complete with a bucket of pony nuts and an array of ropes, the boys were reluctant to listen to reason. They continued to take huge delight in racing up and down the hill in a manic game of 'chase me', the fun of which had deserted most of the pursuants seconds after its initiation, and it was some time before the fugitives were prepared to give in and come quietly.

The long talked of removal of the ponies to new pastures for the winter, suddenly became a top priority, none of us wishing to see a repeat of recent shenanigans, and two days later the ponies were walked down the hill to the village, where they could be 'kept an eye on' more easily. In the circumstances, with myself out of action, this was probably all for the good, though we hoped to see them back in the spring if we could improve their fencing, as they had done an excellent job of keeping the grass down.

~

Of course, Murphy's Law states that when you are barely struggling to hold things together, one crisis after another is bound to follow. It was now, just days before the arrival of the rest of the family for Christmas, that the drains became well and truly blocked. No matter how Brian jiggled the plunger down the pipe, the blockage just would not budge. With all Brian's extra jobs, not to mention recalcitrant chickens, the drain remained blocked for days, leaving the upstairs shower room and loo, as well as the kitchen sink, totally unusable. When he *did* get a chance to tackle the job, we were still no better off, as Brian announced that he had now managed to lose the end of the plunger down the pipe!

Unable to use the dishwasher or the kitchen sink, we were now reduced to washing up in the bath. The inconvenience and extra hassle made everything such a chore. Simple tasks like making a cup of tea, weren't simple any more, and night-time hikes to the downstairs bathroom left us cold and unable to get back to sleep again, making everyone irritable and fed up.

Washing up in the bath with one hand was not without its difficulties, not to mention laboriously slow, so only the most essential items were processed thus. By Christmas Eve the dishwasher was full to bursting with dirty dishes & cutlery, as was the draining board, and we had not a single clean plate to eat off. There was a chocolate log to make and a ham to boil, not to mention the turkey to prepare, veg to chop and a house full of people all needing the bathroom. Christmas was on the point of being cancelled; things couldn't continue as they were. With tempers frayed, Sam decided to add his muscle to the drain problem, and I decided that this was as good a time as any to slip away and deliver the last of the Christmas cards round the village. As I slid the bar closed on the front gate and made my escape, the air rang with irritable profanities at the back of the house, as the poking and prodding continued anew.

When I returned about an hour later, it was good to hear that progress had finally been made, and that the pipe was now clear of the original blockage. The end of the plunger however, remained stuck in the pipe and out of reach, though possibly now tilted and so allowing *some* water to drain. At least we would now be able to risk using the kitchen sink and the dishwasher, though the upstairs toilet would have to remain out of bounds for a while longer. There was little else we could do with everything now shut for the holiday, but after Christmas we hoped to find someone who would know how best to recover the plunger!

As I couldn't peel potatoes or prepare sprouts, Brian found he had yet *more* jobs to do on Christmas Eve, and by the evening he was utterly exhausted, poor thing. I, on the other hand, had the most relaxing Christmas ever, having time to sit and watch the full schedule of Christmas movies whilst others took care of the endless preparations in the kitchen.

14. Snow

After Christmas, it was great to have my plaster cast off and be able to get back to looking after the chickens again. I was beginning to regain some movement in my fingers, though my whole hand was really stiff after two weeks of immobilisation. A long programme of physiotherapy and ultrasound treatments lay ahead, but it was so good to feel useful again, and not constantly having to ask Brian if he had remembered to do 'this or that'. It was lovely too, to be back talking to my girls; I'd missed our conversations in the mornings.

Spence, however, was less impressed to see me, and within a week of my return he was intent on demonstrating zero-tolerance towards any hint of my 'cosying-up' to his girls. He took to launching himself feet first at me as soon as I entered the run, and it once again became necessary to take the broom with me on every visit. Having had little trouble with him, myself, for quite some months, though Brian had suffered his wrath over more recent weeks, this was a disappointing deterioration in our relationship and it was clear bridges needed rebuilding.

I started taking our German Shepherd, Storm, with me whenever I needed to enter the run, hoping that this might curtail Spence's aggressive lunges, or at least distract him somewhat. However, so inflated was the cockerel's ego, that even the dog had trouble with him, despite the huge difference in size. I suppose, on a positive note, at least I knew he would probably put up a good fight, should we ever have trouble with a fox scaling the fence. Storm, on the other hand, bounded around completely oblivious to Spence's posturing, which you could see irked the bird no end. Storm being such a gentle soul, just couldn't imagine that there could be any kind of issue between Spence and himself, and so with his nose to the ground he snuffled around the chickens, reorganised the log pile (something he was very fond of doing, in an effort to find the best one to carry about with him) or nipped across to say hello to Dot, whose tail tip flicked wildly in annoyance at yet another interrupted hunt.

~

As my hand continued to improve, we got down to some long overdue jobs, urged on by the threat of 'significant amounts of snow' promised for the end of the week. Firstly, we needed to trim the top of the laurel hedge between the road and the front of the house. The view from our bedroom window had become punctuated with several long shoots, which threatened to obscure the much loved panorama of mountain and field, the latter soon to be bustling with newborn lambs. Cutting back the hedge would also serve to keep our phone-line safe from being whipped by stray branches, should the gale-force winds return.

As a Christmas present to ourselves, we had bought a snazzy new saw on an extendable four metre pole, and now came the opportunity to give it a go. It was a tricky job which required both of us with necks craned skyward, to identify the branches that needed cutting and to wield the saw, but before long we had lopped off a full metre from the top of the hedge and were feeling well-satisfied with the results.

Building on the euphoria of finally being able to tick something off the long list of jobs that needed to be completed over the winter months, we moved on to the next: rebuilding the raised beds in the vegetable patch. These had definitely seen better days and were crumbling away with wet rot. We started by moving the enormous, and very heavy, planks that we'd managed to procure from a local sawmill, into the garage. They had been stacked outside for the last couple of months, and would need to dry out thoroughly before we could creosote them. Rebuilding the beds would be a big job, but one that needed completing in the next few weeks if we were going to be ready for the next growing season.

Just two weeks into the new year however, winter arrived. A large accumulation of snow, accompanied by gale force winds, resulted in blizzards and hazardous driving conditions. Many towns and villages were cut off in South and West Wales, and over 10,000 people were left without power. Although passage down our road in a vehicle would have been wholly inadvisable, we did at least have electricity. Most of the snow had arrived in the early hours of the morning, and by first light the electric fences around the two chicken runs were a good 20cm deep in snow, more in places where it had drifted. The green lights on the energisers though, continued to wink at us, leading us to believe that the fences were live and effective.

The ferocious wind whipped the snow up from the field and hurled it at the end of the house, covering all the windows and doors on the south side of the property in a white render of ice. Every tree, post and wall was 'painted' on its southerly flank, creating spectacular outlined landscapes, barely visible through the mist of ice particles that continued to be thrust horizontally across the fields.

I donned my wellies, grabbed my bucket, a spade and some layers pellets and set off into the wilderness of white. I bent my head low and pushed forward against the icy flakes as they stung my face, my feet cutting channels in the snow as I made my way to the coop on the top field. On opening the coop door it was soon clear that the chickens and Spence were not at all impressed by the adverse weather conditions, and if I thought they were coming out, then I could think again. I tipped the food into the feeder, only to be thanked with a jab to the back of my hand from Spence, who was clearly not in the best of moods. I did my best to clean around the milling feet, keeping a wary eye on the cockerel. With the coop clean and the water freed of ice, I turned my attention to clearing the electric fence. I started by working my way around the inside of the electric netting with the spade, aiming to tackle the outside of the fence on my second circuit. However, by the time I had made it around the 50 metre fence, the place where I had begun was again heaped with snow, my futile efforts now totally erased. I admitted defeat and made my way down to the young chickens on the lower field. They too were surrounded by quite a depth of snow, and equally reluctant to venture out. In fact, as it turned out, little was seen of any of the chickens all day.

It was only about half an hour before dusk that one of the young chickens, obviously desperate for a drink before bed, intrepidly ventured from the coop. The snow however, was deeper and colder than she had at first anticipated, and she soon found herself literally up to her neck. Bravely, after only a short pause, she pushed on finally managing to make it to the drinker. However, she appeared to be far too traumatised to even contemplate the return journey, and she sat huddled over her feet in an effort to keep warm. Fortunately for her, I had spotted her dilemma and headed out to affect a rescue, scooping her up in my arms and returning her to the warmth of the coop; with the icy wind and falling overnight temperatures, she would surely have died had she remained where she was.

By the following morning the wind had dropped and we were just left with the snow. The lane from the village remained treacherous, and only the bravest of souls with four-wheel-drive vehicles attempted to negotiate it. Walkers were another thing though, and we were delighted to find a string of friends popping in for coffee and a warm by the fire. With the visitors came news as to the depth of snow in other parts of the village and interesting anecdotes of madcap plans. Apparently a snowplough, in attempting to clear a route over the mountain, had become stuck on one of the notoriously steep roads just across the river from us. A second snowplough, which had come to the rescue, had then managed to overturn in the ditch and completely block the road, making it impassable for the foreseeable future.

With the wind calmed and no new snow forecast for the next 24 hours, I set about digging out the electric fences again. By the end of the afternoon both chicken runs had fully cleared electric fences and the batteries had been recharged. Although we hadn't seen any evidence of fox prints in the snow, we felt it was only a matter of time before hunger brought one our way, looking for an easy meal. The weight of the snow and ice on the electric netting had caused it to sag in quite a few places, and we felt we had probably been very lucky to escape an attack thus far.

By the next day, the chickens seemed to be getting used to the white stuff and ventured outside a bit more. Following the intrepid young chicken's experience, I thought it best to clear a path from the coop to the water in both runs, and the girls seemed glad to be able to get out in the fresh air at last. There had been several squabbles the previous day, in both coops, as living in such close quarters frayed the nerves. None of the chickens strayed far though, and indeed most spent their time beneath the coops, aimlessly standing and looking across the run at the snow. In an effort to distract them from further squabbles, I hung some old sprout stalks in each run for them to peck at. Though there seemed only a passing interest in the greenery to start with, a few hours later they were completely devoid of leaves and all that remained were the thick, fibrous stems.

Storm had a totally different attitude to the snow, and thought it was the best thing he'd ever seen. He couldn't wait to come out with me, and he pranced and pounced, and ran for the sheer joy of it, snuffling his nose into the drifts and daring me to chase him. He even managed to seek out some of Brian's logs beneath the snow and 'rescue' them. Dot was less enamoured with the change in the weather, and picked her way daintily through the shallower bits. Her favourite spot became the end of the coffee table in the lounge, where she could sit just a short distance from the patio doors, with a perfect view of all the garden birds that were now feeding on the seed I had scattered for them. She stared out at them making staccato meows, as all cats seem to do when they see a bird. Sometimes she forgot that she was inside and would lean towards the door, coiled and ready to pounce, before remembering, just in the nick of time, that there was in fact a huge pane of glass between her and her prey. She also enjoyed the extra warmth from the woodburner, that was now lit from early morning until late at night, in an effort to stave off the cold.

~

As January passed into February, the snow melted away. The winds though, chased around the house and whistled through any gaps in the doors and windows they could find. Despite the raw chill wrought by the wind, it was good to see some bright sunny days and have a chance to tackle a few more of the winter jobs on our list.

131

One of those jobs was to prepare a run for the pigs that we hoped to get in March. Having pigs had been one of Brian's long held dreams, and at last the time had come when we felt confident enough to give it a go. Luckily the boys and I had bought him several good books on the subject, which proved practical and a good source of information. We were also very fortunate in having several neighbours who kept pigs themselves, and who, true to form, were only too pleased to share their knowledge and time with us.

As one of the main aims of having pigs was to clear the lower field of tussocks, reeds and brambles, we decided that we would place the pig house in the centre of the field and rotate the run around this in a clock-like fashion. This way we would not have to move the house each time we moved the pigs onto a new patch. We discovered, through our research, that 3 wires were needed on our newly purchased electric fence, at heights of roughly 15cm, 25cm and 40cm. Luckily we had also made the decision to buy three winding-reels when purchasing the electric fencing kit, so we could easily wind up any excess wire. Unfortunately the kit we had purchased however, which should have come with three rolls of 200 metres, arrived with two rolls of 400 metres. Although we had ended up with an extra 200 metres of wire, we found ourselves compelled to measure out three lengths of 200 metres to put on the winding-reels, which is not as easy as it might sound. For one, when unrolled in lengths of more than a couple of metres, the wire is inclined to kink. For another, 200 metres is a lot to count without losing your place. To perform this incredible feat, we chose to work in the comfort of the lounge, using the two metre width of the lounge rug as our measuring guide. Brian sat on a chair at one side of the rug with one of the 400 metre reels of wire, desperately trying to prevent loops of wire escaping from the reel with his foot, and I stood on the other side of the rug turning the winding-reel and walking across the rug towards him counting two metres at a time. It was a long and laborious task, which had to be repeated monotonously until we had the 200 metres of wire wound onto each of the winding-reels. Amazingly, we only lost count once, and that was on the last reel, which may or may not be two metres longer than the other two, but as it was the last reel and we were past caring by then, we downed tools and put the kettle on.

Luckily, the following week the weather took a turn for the better and we were at last able to prepare the run for the pigs. Although we hoped the pigs would clear the land of brambles for us, we felt the huge patch along the stream side of the field, might be a bit much for two little eight-week-old weaners. We had visions of the poor little things emerging from the thicket with a mass of nasty gashes across their backs, leading to infections and expensive visits by the vet. So we spent two long days clearing them ourselves by hand. Our arms and legs throbbed with copious scratches, despite wearing gloves and thick jeans. It was a soul destroying job, cutting each individual bramble stalk and tugging it free from the tangled mass. Even worse than the brambles were the briars that grew amongst them, and whose thorns were ten times as sharp. It somehow became *my* responsibility to grab the thorny bundles of cut material and carry them up the field to the bonfire, walking sideways with legs apart in order to avoid the wands of prickles from attaching themselves to my inner thighs, and my head leaning to one side in an effort to avoid my face from being mutilated. Unfortunately this generally proved fruitless, as suckers invariably wrapped themselves around every extremity. It was one job that we were very glad to tick off the list, and we treated ourselves to a bar of chocolate to celebrate its completion as we recovered exhausted and torn to bits.

A few days later, John, who each year kept a couple of pigs himself, arrived with an old wooden crate and some pallets that he thought we could cobble together into a house for our pigs. As we proudly showed him the newly cleared area for our pigs, he could barely conceal his mirth. Our two days of bramble clearing had, in his opinion, been a total waste of time, as the little pigs it seemed would have relished the chance to tackle the job. This revelation stung, but not quite as much as our still smarting wounds.

The following day Chloe and her partner Rob arrived with their sledge hammer, to help us bang a post into the ground which would hold the reels of electric wire for the pig fence. With Brian's back suffering from several days of bramble bashing, Rob decided to wield the sledgehammer for us. The fact that Rob had never wielded a sledgehammer in his life before didn't seem to be a problem, in his eyes anyway, until that is, he raised it over his shoulder and the weight and momentum took hold and sent him staggering backwards. Whoops of hilarity and banter soon had the rest of us weak with hysterical laughter. However, with Rob's noble determination, and very little help from the rest of us, the job was done and we retired to the house for tea and cake.

15. Lessons

The next couple of weeks proved to be a busy time, and not just on the smallholding. I was due to attend my niece's wedding in Eire and there were certain jobs we needed to get done before I left. Our prime focus was the replacement of the two raised beds at the bottom of the vegetable garden, which were both in a pretty rotten state, with one very large raised bed. We had already moved some of the new twelve foot planks into the garage to dry, and now we set about coating them with creosote. Carrying each chunky batch of planks in and out of the garage was no easy task with my hand still not back to full strength after my accident, and Brian's back still causing him some problems. However, it's amazing how determination and an imminent deadline can spur you on, and shortly before my planned departure we had the frame completed. Being on a hillside plot, it stood three planks high at the bottom side of the slope and two planks on the upper most edge. It looked a good sturdy job that we hoped would last for many seasons. The only problem I could see with it, was that this bed was a lot deeper than the two beds it had replaced, and there simply wouldn't be enough soil to fill it. More than a few bags of seaweed and barrow loads of compost, courtesy of the ducks, geese and chickens, would be needed in order to bring the level up to where it needed to be.

Brian was a great believer in the use of seaweed to improve the soil, and we had gathered many bags from the nearby beaches since our arrival at Nantcoed. However, we were about to embark on one seaweed gathering excursion that would remain etched in our brains forever; a nightmare trip that neither of us would ever wish to repeat.

Whilst I wandered off along the beach to hunt for interesting pieces of driftwood, Brian spent his time bagging up several old feed-sacks with seaweed. We loaded the bulging bags into the boot of the car and set off for home. However, before we had travelled more than half a mile, it was evident that we had interlopers. Hundreds of tiny black flies poured out of the seaweed bags behind us and enveloped the car's interior. What started as a few flies on the windscreen, soon escalated to a swarm of epic proportions. The windscreen being covered in a veil of black dots, and the constant swatting and swiping employed by the driver, threatened to plunge us headlong into the nearest ditch. We pulled up at some temporary traffic lights, wound down the windows and scrolled back the sunroof. Clouds of small black flies issued from each opening, but still there seemed just as many flies swarming around our faces. Checking the rear-view mirror, I caught sight of a white transit van behind us, and could only imagine what the driver was thinking; it must have looked extremely suspicious, as if perhaps we were disposing of a dead body! As we pulled away from the lights, the flies were everywhere...up our noses, in our ears, and, if we were stupid enough to speak, in our mouths. I pushed my foot to the floor, hoping to cover the 20 minute journey in a fraction of the time. With mouths held tight shut, sign language was the only communication available to us between swats to left and right. Of course we could have stopped and dumped the seaweed (complete with flies), but this option would not be entertained by Brian, who had laboured hard to collect the offending seaweed. When we eventually swerved into the drive and screeched to a stop (having abandoned the planned stop off at the supermarket), we both fell out of the car almost before the engine had stopped, and shook the flies from our hair and clothes. I left it to Brian to unload the bags and air the car. He tipped the seaweed into the raised bed, but it was clear we would need a lot more if we were to even come close to filling it.

Two days later, we were back collecting seaweed again.

'There won't be any flies this time,' declared Brian confidently, 'It's far too cold.'

However, as soon as we stepped onto the beach it was all too plain that the seaweed was crawling with flies. Luckily Brian was ready for them this time (despite being supposedly convinced that there wouldn't be any); he had brought a length of string and a penknife, so that he could tie the bags closed, and so prevent any repeat of the previous fiasco. I left him to it and went in search of more driftwood.

On my return to the car, Brian was tying the bags tightly shut and loading them, upside down, into the back of the car.

'That'll sort them,' he declared confidently.

'We'll see,' I replied.

Well, we had barely travelled a mile before the first fly buzzed past my left cheek, and a glance in the rear-view mirror revealed a growing mass of bugs peppering the back window. Admittedly, this journey was not in any way as horrendous as the previous one, but it was still pretty unpleasant all the same. Closer examination of the bags later revealed a mass of pinprick holes in each bag, just big enough for the flies to limbo through. Not willing to risk putting ourselves through further bug infested trips, all seaweed collecting was abandoned until further notice, and so work on the new raised bed was temporarily suspended.

With a disappointing return to Arctic weather conditions a few days later, our two ponds became topped with a thin layer of ice, trapping the recently laid frogspawn in speckled mounds. At least with the ground frozen, the mud in the chicken runs became a little easier to negotiate. The wear and tear of eighteen chickens intent on scarifying the grass to within an inch of its life in the run on the bottom field was becoming beyond a joke, and the run on the hill wasn't a lot better. I decided the only answer was to let the chickens out to free-range around the garden, in the hope that the muddy patches would have a chance to repair themselves.

To start with, the young chickens were not convinced that this was such a good idea, and stubbornly continued to paddle about in familiar surroundings. After a week of leaving their gate open however, I lost hope of them ever finding their way out and unceremoniously hoisted each one over the fence. Once out, they soon decided that they rather liked it. In fact, on the days we were going out for the day and therefore didn't want the chickens loose about the place, they looked for every opportunity to slip past me at the gate and escape into the garden. The older chickens were less reticent and were thrilled from the start to be given the opportunity to wander across the field and scratch through the rough grass for tasty morsels.

To start with the two groups of chickens chose to stay well clear of each other, with the youngsters 'bagsying' the front lawn under the dining room window, and the patio. Unfortunately this area also included one of our small ponds, and with chickens prone to moments of incredible dimness, it was only a matter of time before one small group was seen venturing directly across the thin ice that coated the pond's surface.

From the dining room window, we held our breath.

Incredibly, despite staying in a tight pack, and therefore making no attempt to spread their combined weight in order to reduce the risk, they ambled aimlessly across to the other side, totally oblivious of their amazing good fortune.

Our relief was short-lived however, as later the same day the youngsters took themselves out of the front gate and up the lane. With true chicken logic, they picked one of the two times in the day that our lane could be remotely called 'busy': the afternoon 'school-run' (the other time being the morning 'school-run'). Luckily, the breakout was spotted relatively quickly, and delays to travellers were kept to a minimum as I shepherded the group back down the lane and into the drive.

Now that the youngsters had discovered that they could climb through the bars on the front gate, some chicken-proofing was urgently required. Discovering a roll of plastic mesh at the back of the garage, I carefully tied a strip to the lower part of the gate, to deter any squeezing through, or limboing under, the gate. Then I painted a sign, which I wired to the top of the gate: 'PLEASE SHUT THE GATE, BEAUTIFUL BUT NOT VERY STREETWISE CHICKENS ON THE LOOSE'.

It did the trick, and prevented any further excursions out onto the lane. The only downside was the over diligence of passers-by, who, on seeing the gate open at any point, even when the chickens *weren't* loose in the garden, would kindly close it. So, if it was raining hard and one or other of us had decided to use the car to nip down to the shop to collect the paper, leaving the gate open briefly, we'd often return to a closed gate, resulting in a soaking as we dashed to unlatch it again, which really rather defeated the whole purpose of taking the car in the first place! This happened with surprising frequency, our lovely postman being one of the main culprits; such thoughtfulness was heart-warming and it was lovely to know that everyone was looking out for the safety of our chickens, so we learnt to bear the soakings with relative good humour... most of the time.

Despite the freezing weather, we were pleasantly surprised to find a significant improvement in the number of eggs we were now getting. Our eight older girls had gone into overdrive and were producing an egg each most days. This was the best output we'd ever had; better even than the summer months. The youngsters however, appeared to be struggling to maintain their initial good rate of lay. We'd had the odd soft-shelled egg, as we had done with our original girls when they first came into lay, but I wondered whether all the free-ranging they were now getting had put them off their stride somewhat. I kept my eyes peeled in the garden, just in case anyone had been caught-short, but no stray eggs came to light.

As both groups of chickens became more confident in their free-ranging, they periodically merged; sometimes intentionally, but often unintentionally as a result of mistaken identity. With the sudden realisation that they were in fact standing next to a stranger and not one of their group of chums, there followed the briefest of pauses (that OMG moment) before an undignified scrap ensued. It was the youngsters that appeared, with their teenage disregard for all authority and proper etiquette, to be at the top of the pecking order, and they showed their mothers little or no respect. The brazen juveniles mounted regular raids on the hillside coop, pillaging their water and food (which of course tasted *far* superior to theirs, despite being from the same tap and sack as their own). After several weeks of tolerating such bad behaviour, the older girls finally retaliated, launching their own raid on the youngsters' coop, causing the situation to escalate rapidly.

On nipping down the garden to fetch the wheelbarrow one afternoon, I noticed that one of the youngsters was missing. An extensive search of the garden was mounted but this proved fruitless, and I started to wonder if she'd strayed too far and been lost to the fox. However, further investigations revealed that she had actually taken up squatter's rights in the 'granny annexe' on the hill. On opening the lid, I was greeted with nervous stares from the interloper, her eyes constantly checking the door lest she be discovered enjoying the luxury of somebody else's prime laying location. Having already collected eight eggs from the eight older girls, this ninth egg revealed one important fact... our recent tallying of laying rates in each coop was now clearly 'up the spout'.

My short trip across to the west coast of Ireland with my Mum, for the wedding of my niece was now just days away, and one crucial job still remained. With Spence now exhibiting a frightening escalation in his aggression towards Brian and myself, a tough decision had to be made. Over the preceding few weeks and months, entering the chicken run on the hill had only become possible with a broom in hand and a partner standing by to launch a rescue mission, should it be required. It was a situation that had become intolerable, and with my impending departure we both knew the time had come to reclaim control. Spence would have to go, and being too dangerous to pass on to anyone else there was only one option. Brian fetched the landing net. I was concerned that the girls should not see Spence's demise, thinking they might be upset to witness the death of their lover, so the plan was to do all we could to shield them from our actions. We entered the run, leaving the gate ajar, and advanced on Spence. With his natural desire to sink his spurs into our thighs, there was no chasing required, and a swift sweep of the net captured the aggressor instantly. We firmly pinned him to the ground in an effort to avoid his penetrating jabs. I glanced over my shoulder to gauge the girls' fragile emotional state. I need not have worried, as, excited by the prospect of a day free-ranging in the garden, they hiked off through the gate in ebullient high spirits without a backward glance, and Spence drew his last breath.

'They're sure to miss him come bedtime,' I said. But as dusk wrapped the hillside in tones of grey and the girls filed back to their coop, there appeared to be very little interest as to their leader's whereabouts. Not only that, but the following morning there was a distinct aura of relief as the girls managed to emerge for once, unscathed by over-amorous advances. Poor

Spence, his overzealous dedication to duty had not endeared him to those he'd stoically fought to protect.

With safety in the chicken run now restored, I felt confident in leaving Brian in sole-charge of the smallholding for a few days, as I attended what turned out to be a really good Irish 'knees-up'.

Mum and I caught the train to Birmingham Airport and checked in, allowing plenty of time to negotiate airport security. Past experience had alerted us all, as a family, to this precaution whenever travelling with Mum by plane. Over the years, there had been several notable incidents, the most renowned (and the grandchildren's favourite) being the one when she was stopped from taking a hand-grenade on board a plane to Knock, in the west of Eire - and this at the height of the troubles in Northern Ireland! Admittedly, it was only a plastic hand-grenade, which she hoped would be the perfect accompaniment to the little camouflage suit she'd bought for her grandson, but a hand-grenade nonetheless. As she had only spotted it in a shop on the way to the airport, she had popped it into her handbag and thought no more about it. Of course, at airport security there was great alarm when they discovered the device concealed in her hand-luggage, and this smart looking, mature lady was whisked off for further interrogation. The hand-grenade was of course confiscated, lest this Grandmother of ten should think of deploying it in an attempt to hijack the plane. My lovely Mum was mortified, but she has given us many chuckles over the years when taking flights abroad, and happy banter abounds with every new trip as to what she'll be stopped for next. We imagine her to be on one of those 'most wanted' lists, and that CCTV cameras are on high alert as she carries a variety of toys through the scanners, some with ambiguous shapes or suspicious batteries and wiring enclosed, and one, if my memory serves me correctly, that started playing Brahms' lullaby as her suitcase disappeared down the conveyor-belt at check-in. However, on this occasion, the trip was totally incident free and we sailed through security in both directions. It was a fabulous few days, and a welcome break from all the chores.

16. Pigs

Brian had done a sterling job whilst I was away, keeping the smallholding ticking over, and for once, the chickens had behaved themselves too. It was now 'full steam ahead' for our pig project.

With the imminent arrival of our weaners, we were spurred on to get the pig shelter completed. A length of 'damp proof membrane' was purchased, and a whole day was spent covering the wooden crate, first with the plastic membrane, and then with some heavy duty, and very appropriately named, pig wire. Personally, I felt that chicken wire would have done a better job, having smaller gaps between the wires as well as being far easier to bend. However, Brian had other ideas and was determined to use some wire fencing that he had found amongst the patch of brambles we'd cleared. As the purpose of the wire was to dissuade the pigs from chewing and pulling the plastic off the house, I felt the wire fencing, with snout-sized gaps between the wires, wouldn't quite be up to the job, but I knew better than to argue, as when Brian gets an idea in his head he is rarely swayed. Time would no doubt tell if his choice had been the right one. The pig wire was immensely difficult to manoeuvre, and tricky to bend around the corners of the crate. Eventually though, it was done and the little house just needed its corrugated iron roof to finish the job. This we tied on with strong rope, strapping it at the sides to the pig wire. The inside was filled with plenty of fresh straw and at last we were ready to receive our pigs.

Sourcing a couple of weaners however, was not as easy as we'd anticipated. Our friend and neighbour, John, had given us the mobile number of a pig farmer who had supplied him in the past, and who was likely to have piglets of the right age. Unfortunately, although Brian rang the number every day for a week, he seemed unable to get hold of him. Eventually I checked the internet and found the farmer's landline, which Brian rang for two more days without response. When he finally did manage to make contact, it was with the chap's mother, and she promised to pass the message on and get someone to call us back that evening. However, the call did not materialise and we started to consider looking for another supplier. It was not until the following morning (Easter Sunday!) that the phone rang, and we were told that they did, indeed, have some eight-week-old weaners, but that if we wanted them, we'd have to collect them that day, as they had a hectic week ahead of them, moving sheep. Without an appropriate vehicle with which to transport pigs, and having no idea exactly where the pig farm was, we phoned John who had promised to come with us when we got our weaners, as he wanted some too.

As it happened, the timing for John and his wife, Julie, could not have been worse, as they had been up all night with one of their goats, bringing twins through a difficult breach birth. On top of this, it was the start of British Summertime and those of us who hadn't actually lost the *whole* night's sleep, had at least lost an hour of it; so nobody was on their best form. But, typical of our friends, all they required was time to grab some breakfast, and within the hour they were at our gate with their big red transit van. With only room for three of us in the front, Brian volunteered to travel in the back of the van, and we threw him some cushions to compensate for the poor suspension and lack of seating. With no windows in the back, and the roar of the engine drowning out all conversation, poor Brian had no inkling of where exactly we were, and he clutched tightly to the edge of a modest opening in the metalwork that divided the rear body from the cab, trying to glean what information he could as we sped down narrow lanes on the way to the farm.

As it had been a year since John had been to the pig farm, and then only via a round-about route as directed by a mate, I had brought along my SATNAV (or SAT NAG, as Julie called it). John however, in his wisdom, decided from the start to antagonise the lady on the SATNAV by heading off in the opposite direction, activating innumerable calls to 'recalculate'. However, her revenge was sweet when, somewhere close to where we were heading, she chose to send us 'off road' and the pink line on the screen started to track alarmingly across fields, in preference to tarmac. After bouncing uncontrollably (particularly poor Brian in the back, who had little he could safely grab hold of) down a potholed track, we arrived at a farm, though unfortunately not the right one. John jumped out and went in search of someone who could give us directions. When he eventually returned and expertly manoeuvred the van through a three-point-turn in a very confined space, the SATNAV asked, 'Would you like to use Pedestrian mode?'

'No!' we all chorused, none more enthusiastically than Brian!

After just one more false turn, and directions from a chap in a mini digger, we bounced along what must have been one of the longest drives in Ceredigion, peppered with even bigger potholes than the previous track, to finally arrive at our destination. Sliding the side door of the van open, we quickly released Brian, who stepped out into the daylight, slightly dishevelled and a little dazed, but in a remarkably good state, all things considered.

Unfortunately, having finally arrived, it turned out that they only had two weaners, and not the ninety odd we'd all expected. John and Julie generously agreed that we should have these two, and that they would source theirs elsewhere. On entering the barn we were faced with two of the cutest piglets, one boy and one girl. Having discussed our options on the journey over, John had advised us to get either two boys or two girls, but had warned us to avoid having one of each. However, now faced with exactly that option, we were told it probably wouldn't be a problem. The pigs were ear-tagged and the paperwork completed. Soon our weaners were loaded into a crate in the back of the van, with Brian settled on his cushions alongside, and we were back on the road.

The return journey was much less eventful, and a great deal less bumpy, as our driver this time decided to follow the SATNAV from start to finish, ensuring we kept tarmac beneath our tyres all the way home. Before long the van pulled up by our field gate, and the two little pigs were unceremoniously carried by their back legs and plonked in the middle of the run we had made for them.

These pigs however, had never seen the great outdoors before, having been reared in a small pen inside a barn, and the sheer expanse of open space they now found themselves surrounded by proved a revelation to them. They hurtled full speed across the run, one of them managing to shoot straight through the electric fence. Within moments of arriving, these little porkers had three of us chasing across the field after them. John, Brian and I dodged and lunged, tripping headfirst over tussocks of grass whilst the piglets bolted this way and that evading each desperate attempt to grab them. Meanwhile, Julie stood, beside herself with laughter, as the frenetic scene unravelled before her.

As it turned out, this was to be just one escape amongst many that afternoon. Having eventually managed to return the runaways to their enclosure, John and Julie beat a hasty retreat, and left us to it. It wasn't long though before we were doing the dodging, lunging and tripping thing all over again, as our piglets continued to take great delight in rushing straight through the fence, despite the zaps they were getting each time. We'd obviously got a couple of adrenalin junkies on our hands.

Between these energetic bouts, our little pigs collapsed in an exhausted heap amongst the marsh reeds and slept - heavily. In fact they slept so heavily that they didn't even hear us approaching, and we found that we could gently stroke their backs as they snoozed. We had been advised that it was a good idea to get our pigs used to human company, as this would make raising them much easier all round. When awake, the youngsters were far too fast and unpredictable though, to get anywhere near them; a fact confirmed when later that evening, we felt we should 'persuade' them into their little house and out of the biting easterly wind. With Sam home from uni, there were three of us to creep up on the pigs, who were lying just in front of the doorway. It seemed but a simple matter to coax them inside, and you'd think there was little chance of failure with them already positioned so close to the door. However, as soon as the pigs awoke and realised they were surrounded, they bolted straight between us. Sam sailed horizontally through the air, arms fully extended in an impressive rugby tackle, his hands just missing one pair of trotters as they raced past him. Failing dismally, we decided to abort the mission and retire to the house, hoping that the pigs would work it out for themselves when the temperature dropped still further overnight.

The following morning, Brian was awake early and peering out of the bedroom window to see if he could see his pigs. To our relief they were still inside their fence and, despite spending the night outside their house in sub-zero temperatures, they were still alive. On this second day, we decided our strategy would be to keep the pigs as calm as possible; in other words, we wouldn't *make* them do anything they didn't want to. That way, we hoped to avoid any escapes, and that our pigs would feel so secure that they would venture inside their house of their own free will.

The day was thankfully devoid of the drama endured the previous day, and the plan seemed to be working, but when Brian went down to give the pigs their supper at 7pm they were nowhere to be seen. He shouted up the field to me, where I was shutting the chickens away for the night.

'They're gone! I can't see them anywhere!'

As he shouted, a tiny, barely audible, grunt came from deep inside the pig house. We peered inside, but there was no sign of the pigs at all. As we stared nonplussed at the empty space, a small patch of straw gently rose and fell, rhythmically inhaling and exhaling. We crept away, so as not to disturb them, relieved to know that our piglets had at last seen sense and sort shelter from the predicted overnight temperatures of -4°C.

The following morning Brian was up early again to feed the pigs, who he imagined would be ravenous after having missed their supper the night before. He called, rattled the bucket and tipped their food into the feeder, but not a snout or a trotter did as much as twitch in the depths of the pig house. Following two traumatic and high-spirited days of escaping, a lie-in was obviously called for. In fact it was well after 9am when the piglets finally emerge from their hut!

Having eventually dragged themselves from their bed, the youngsters wasted no time at all in making for their breakfast, and they even seemed happy to approach us a little, though ensuring they remained just out of touching distance. However, by the end of the day, and after several bonding sessions in the pig pen, we actually managed to stroke them as they tucked into their food. The little boar was much more up for having his back scratched than the gilt, but with a great deal of patience, she eventually came round to the idea that a little human interaction might be quite pleasant. The pig pen was thankfully beginning to exude an air of peace and contentment.

Twenty four hours later our new arrivals were most definitely feeling more at home, as they chased each other around like playful puppies, nudging each other into action. This was almost always initiated by the little boar, whose mischievous character was now coming to the fore. The gilt appeared to be above such antics, but tolerated her brother's enthusiasm for games and, when it suited, she allowed herself to join in with the high-jinks of youthful horseplay. These energetic interludes though were generally short lived, and were most often followed by a long sleep in the sun - two long pink bodies, side by side and nose to tail, like two giant sausages tucked amongst the marsh grass, or against the side of their little house, sheltered from the cold East wind.

A few days after acquiring our pigs we had a phone call from John and Julie. They had found some more weaners and had just collected a couple for themselves. They had decided to do a 'whey run' and wondered if we would be interested in accompanying them, so they could show us the ropes. We dropped what we were doing in the garden and prepared ourselves to be picked up in the red van. When he arrived, John came bearing gifts; he'd brought an old shower tray with him that he said we could use as a water trough for our pigs if we'd like. Up to now our pigs had had to make do with quite a deep terracotta garden pot, sunk into the ground and filled to the brim so their little snouts could reach the water, but it was perilously deep should any piglet over-balance and fall in, and necessitated copious trips down the field to keep it topped up. The shower tray would be a far more suitable, and Health & Safety conscious option, being shallow enough for them to reach the water without the danger of drowning, as well as being difficult to tip over.

'The whey run' turned out to be gloriously simple. Across the valley, and no more than two miles from us, we discovered there was a small farm where they made Caerphilly cheese. We drove into the yard and pulled up outside an old stone dairy. On the wall in front of us, was a large switch and a long length of plastic tubing, which snaked its way around the corner of the building. Nobody was about, but John flicked the switch on whilst I was instructed to hold the end of the tube in the neck of one of the large plastic containers he had brought with him. With the turn of a tap, fitted half way along the tube, the whey spurted into the container. Before long we had two containers full, and we loaded them into the van. It all seemed very easy – and all for free too! Apparently every pig owner in the district collected whey from there. Whey, so we were told, was loved by pigs and helped them to put on weight, though an excess, we were warned, could result in too much fat on the finished carcass.

Our pigs hadn't heard about whey being a favourite, and viewed it with great suspicion. We poured some into an upturned dustbin lid, where it remained for a couple of days, being circumnavigated and snorted at regularly. Until that is, someone was eventually brave enough to actually taste it. The yellowish liquid was rolled across the tongue, its 'bouquet' analysed and a second opinion sought. The verdict was a surprisingly palatable offering, with overtones of ripened sock; a 'must-have' for any discerning pig. From this point on, the daily dustbin lid of whey was greeted with huge enthusiasm and squeals of delight.

Now we just had to convince our pigs that 'greens' were equally as appetising. The more 'free' food we could give them, the cheaper our meat would be. The pigs were happy to eat the grass and root up the weeds and tussocks, but had shown very little interest in any 'kitchen scraps' we had offered them. However, we had been warned that acclimatisation to new foodstuffs could take a while, and following our experience with the whey we decided to persevere. In addition to all these 'goodies', we fed our pigs a 50/50 mix of pig pellets and rolled barley which they tucked into enthusiastically. It was the first thing they looked for on emerging from their house in the morning, even before having a wee; and that first wee of the morning was quite something. After a quick intake of fuel they would go over and stand in the marsh grass and wee...and wee...and wee....for what amounted to several minutes. Pigs, contrary to popular belief, are very clean animals, using just one spot as their latrine. Not once did our pair make any mess in their house, and no 'cleaning out' was required; one small bale of straw to plump up their bed, was all that was needed throughout the whole of their stay with us.

A few weeks after our pigs arrived our friends, Chloe and Rob, asked us what we'd called our pigs. Following our policy of 'not naming anything that we planned to eat', we informed our friends that the pigs would remain nameless. This was greeted with horror and we were informed that no animal should ever go without a name. Repeated badgering from our friends eventually saw our pigs being christened Rob and Chloe, just for the sake of a quiet life. However, this actually caused us quite a few chuckles over the coming months, when relaying to each other what we'd seen Rob doing to Chloe, or vice versa.

~

Whilst we still had our youngest son home from university, and not wishing to aggravate Brian's fragile back, I asked Sam to help me move the older chicken coop further up the hill, to a fresh patch of grass. Moving their coop every three months had helped to avoid problems with parasites, as well as preventing any single patch of grass from getting too worn. I also took the opportunity to give the coop a good clean and sprayed it for the dreaded red-mite, which thankfully we had not yet suffered, but which could be quite detrimental to the health of the birds. Red-mites have a habit of hiding in the tiny nooks and crevices of coops, particularly the wooden ones (which both mine were), and feeding on the blood of the chickens at night. With a view to controlling the red-mites and worms, twice a year I also gave the girls a spot of medication on the back of their necks. I had treated the youngsters a couple of weeks previous, with no problem at all; being so tame they'd let me pick them up without any problem. However, the older girls were another case altogether.

149

When I first acquired the older girls, it had been easy to distinguish one from another and I had lovingly named each individual chicken (Rob and Chloe would have been proud). Since their winter moult however, their colouring had altered, and they now all had exactly the same pale buff colour, making identification pretty well impossible. The older girls were also not fond on being handled, making the job additionally challenging. The plan was to catch and treat each bird before popping it over the fence. That way we would know who had been treated, and who was still to treat. It was a plan that we had employed previously with this group, and with a great deal of success.

Everyone was briefed and in position. I had the medication ready in my pocket and was talking calmly to the chickens in an effort to keep everything relaxed. Brian was poised with the landing net ready to whisk it over any chicken that bolted past him, and Sam, renowned for his sporting prowess and skills on the cricket field, was ready, knees bent and poised for any catches and slips that came his way. The chickens, aware that something was up, owing to the number of humans littering their run, were alert and immediately on their guard. We closed in on our first victim, who flung her head through one of the small holes in the netting expecting the rest of her body to follow. Of course it didn't, and she became completely entangled, with her wings and legs making it through a variety of other holes. It took three of us quite some time to extract her, before she could be treated and released over the fence. She hurried away down the hill, flustered and ruffling her feathers, to find sanctuary amongst the tussocks of the lower field. We turned our attention to our next victim. Shocked at having witnessed the assault on their friend, the necks of all the remaining chickens were at full stretch and eyes agog. We closed in on a group of three, who, in panic launched themselves into the air. On suddenly discovering that they could actually fly, that is exactly what they did, right over the fence. Now we were faced with a dilemma: go after the escapees and risk the rest escaping whilst we're away, or treat the ones we still had contained in the run? We could not let the three escapees join the one chicken we'd already treated, otherwise we would have no chance of identifying which one we'd done, so we chose to pursue the three escapees. They headed for one of the compost heaps and we closed in, Brian with his net, Sam insisting that he was not going to be beaten by a chicken, and me whispering calming blandishments. But they were having none of it, and chickens scattered in all directions as Brian swiped and Sam grabbed to no avail. I ran down the hill to head them off and prevent them reuniting with the one. The shenanigans continued for some minutes, until a couple of lucky swipes of the net and an awesome rugby tackle saw the three safely recaptured.

However, seeing the traumatic capers befalling still more of their friends, and not wishing to wait a moment longer in the run like 'sitting ducks', two more chickens took off over the fence and made for the safety of the bramble patch at the top of the hill. The brambles here formed an expansive swathe at least eight metres deep along the boundary. As Sam approached, one brave chicken, who had made it to the top-most edge of the thicket by now, launched herself into the air in an effort to clear the full thorny expanse in one downhill flight. Amazingly, as chickens are not known for their great flying skills, she very nearly made it, dropping like a stone just a metre short. Now encapsulated by a mass of thorns, she buried her head and couldn't bear to look as Sam and I reached in and pulled the prickly runners from around her. Once extracted, she received her medication and was liberated to join the others that had been 'done'. Eventually, we had all the birds treated and released and the coop moved. Funnily enough, we saw very little of the older girls for the rest of the day, though distant glimpses of feathers being ruffled on the furthest boundary of the lower field, far beyond the pig run, gave away their position, as they recovered from the morning's traumatic events.

As night fell, most of the chickens made their way back to their run, albeit a little further up the hill from where they'd left it that morning. One however, (and there's always one) paced back and forth on the muddy patch where the coop used to stand. Glancing up at the newly positioned coop from time to time, she was absolutely adamant that that was not *her* coop, despite the fact that all her friends were milling in and out of it. It was only after a great deal of coaxing, that she was eventually persuaded through the door, and eight exhausted chickens were put to bed for the night.

The chickens on the lower field however, were not so easy. Whereas the older birds were normally content to be snug on their perches up to an hour before dusk, the youngsters were invariably still partying until nearly 10pm in the summer months, and it was getting to the point where I wanted to go to bed before the chickens! In an attempt to get them locked away at a reasonable hour for once, I lifted one after another into the coop, only to find them slipping out again as soon as my back was turned. I abandoned the task and resigned myself to yet another late night.

17.   A second batch of geese!

I could not believe it! We were actually subjecting ourselves to a second batch of geese! After the exasperating ordeal of the 'gang of four' the previous summer, I had hoped Brian would see sense and avoid geese altogether in the future. I was wrong.

To be fair, it had not been *him* that was subjected to the aggressive jabs, and it had not been *him* that had had to repair the damage they'd caused to the chicken fences or pressure wash the copious amounts of excrement off the patio. His passion for roast goose dinners far exceeded any 'inconveniences' the geese had instigated.

After the success of our first attempts at hatching goose eggs, we felt confident of achieving another good hatch. Our second batch of goose eggs though, proved sadly disappointing, with just one out of the six goslings succeeding in breaking free from its shell. Two of the youngsters died in their shells, possibly due to a lack of humidity in the incubator; which seemed incredible when we considered the high rate of success we had had last time, despite the incubator breaking down and having to keep the eggs warm for a while under a lamp, where the humidity was practically zero. The three other eggs were simply not fertile, and we shouldn't have been surprised by this really, when we remembered how we'd pulled out of the farm drive and chortled at the inept gander 'having his wicked way' whilst facing 180° in the wrong direction atop his mate. The signs had been obvious, if only we'd taken note.

Our dilemma now was that we had just one tiny gosling, and knowing that geese hate being alone, it was plain that he would not thrive unless we could find him some other newly hatched friends. I turned to the internet, but the closest in age I could find, within a sensible travelling distance, were two weeks old. With this the only option open to us, we set off to collect a couple.

On arrival at the farm we were invited into a small barn, where, in the corner pen, about twenty young goslings milled around a large feeder. They looked like giants! The difference between our newly hatched gosling and these two week old goslings was something like the difference between a tennis ball and a cauliflower! We worried for our little gosling trying to integrate with these big boys. However, with no other goslings available locally, and being a solitary gosling not an option, we had little choice but to take some home with us. Brian, thinking only of his stomach, decided that we'd take four, despite my protestations that two would be plenty. I reminded him that one day in the not too distant future we'd be faced with plucking *five* geese, but Brian would still not be swayed.

When we arrived home, the discrepancy in size was startling as we popped them in the pen next to our little fella. Our gosling however, was delighted with the arrival of some playmates and couldn't wait to meet the newcomers. Initially, for his own safety we separated the little gosling from the others with some wire, so they would have time to become acquainted, and he eagerly chattered to them through the mesh. Although the big boys seemed happy to associate with the little one through the wire, when allowed into the same pen, they cruelly jabbed him and made it quite clear that he couldn't be in *their* gang. Sadly, the little gosling hero-worshipped the big boys despite their treatment of him, and he stood next to their huge feet and long legs, with his neck craned skywards calling incessantly, begging to join in. It was heartbreaking to watch. At every opportunity the big boys surrounded him and pecked him mercilessly. It was clear that we could not leave all the goslings together unsupervised, and so he remained in solitary confinement in the corner of the main goose run when we weren't around. Despite everything, the little gosling loved nothing better than for the big boys to sit close to his run, so he could snuggle up close to them from his side of the wire, and when they moved out of sight, around the corner of his little pen, he cried loudly and incessantly, his high-pitched squeak earning him the nickname of Moaning Mini or MM.

With the weather now warm enough, and MM two weeks old, we decided to move the goslings outside to the run by the chalet during the day. The change of scene, we hoped, would give the big boys something other than the little gosling to focus on. We set up a smaller area inside the main run for MM, to keep him safe and allow him to see the others.

At night, all the goslings were brought into the garage where it was warm and safe from predators. The big boys would waddle down the hill, past the pond, across the patio and up the slope into the garage. MM however, whose legs were so much shorter, would be carried, tucked into my jacket and invariably nibbling at my chin. As he got a little older, MM walked (or rather, ran) down to the garage with the others. There were always detours of course, for tasty clumps of grass that could not possibly be ignored, and delicious dandelions that just had to be snapped up as they passed.

One evening however, as the goslings were being brought down from their run, two of the big boys got left behind. Having a fleeting 'senior moment', they simply couldn't quite remember which part of the electric netting opened, and they found themselves in a corner where there was no exit. By the time they were eventually rescued and directed towards the gate, the others had disappeared around the corner. Thinking they were now lost and all alone, a wave of panic sent them careering into the overgrown pond, and without their adult feathers of course, they soon became completely waterlogged and started to sink. Luckily, they thought to pull themselves onto a floating mat of grass, and eventually we managed to persuade the two soggy goslings out of the pond to be reunited with the others.

After three weeks, we still had not managed to fully integrate MM with the rest of the goslings, who, just as bullies on the school playground do, waited until they were sure nobody was watching before launching their attacks on the youngster; only his loud squeals alerting us to his demise. The four bullies would then stand displaying 'butter wouldn't melt' looks of innocence and their best 'it wasn't me' faces. A concerted effort was needed to sort his tormentors out once and for all.

When the goslings came down to the garage that night, I stood alongside the pen for half an hour or so, with a length of thin plastic pipe ready to rap anyone who pecked MM. To start with there was a lot of rapping, but they learned quite quickly the relationship between their actions and the piece of pipe.

By the second night, you could see the bullies thinking about pecking the little one and then looking at the pipe and deciding against it. They weren't exactly being friendly, but at least they weren't hurting him. MM, for his part, sensibly kept a low profile and avoided being near the feeder during any big feeding frenzy. Instead, he just sat facing the wall, pretending he wasn't there.

The following afternoon, we decided that the time had come to try all the goslings out together in the goose run, but without the electric fence on (just in case MM got chased into it); pecks were one thing, but pecks *and* a zap might have been a bit much. Things went surprisingly well. MM didn't pester the big boys, and with plenty of space he was able to stay out of pecking distance, most of the time. The big boys generally tolerated MM, only snapping if he inadvertently got in their way. At last we were seeing real progress, and incredibly, a couple of days later you'd never have known there had ever been a problem! At last MM was an accepted member of their gang; his persistence and determination had paid off. The relief was immense.

A couple of weeks later, with the grass in the goose run nibbled down to very little, we allowed the goslings to roam around the smallholding, as we had with our previous batch of geese. This they loved. Being out and about meant that they could wander in and out of the chicken runs, and pinch any scraps the girls had overlooked. MM particularly enjoyed frequenting the young chickens' run on the lower field. However, these forays often led to him being on the opposite side of the fence to his new found mates, and he would invariably plump for the shortest route. Regularly he would be spotted trying to squeeze himself through the small mesh squares of the fence, and several times a day we'd find ourselves having to administer a rescue.

18.   An endless summer

The Smallholder's Show, at Builth Wells, had always been a favourite day out for us, even when we weren't smallholders. We'd study the different breeds of chicken, consider the possibilities of alpacas and generally fantasise about the day when we might have our own smallholding.

Now it was a reality, and we were inexperienced pig owners, gleaning what advice we could. We compared the sizes and ages of weaners with our own, and attended talks about the feeding and finishing of pigs. We were keen to make a success of keeping our first pigs.

Having discovered how big our pigs should be for their age, we decided to measure them and determine their weight. Being so inexperienced, we had yet to develop the 'knowing eye' that can just look at a pig and know its weight, so we resorted to using a special pig-measuring tape. The tape is passed around the girth of the pig, just behind its shoulders, and the measurement in centimetres is then converted into kilograms with the aid of a simple chart. It sounded a straightforward process, on the face of it, but keeping a pig still long enough to take accurate measurements of its belly, whilst your wellies are stuck in a pit of glutinous mud, was always likely to be fraught with difficulty; careful planning was called for. Lucky for us however, our regular handling of the pigs paid off, and the measurements were thankfully achieved with surprising ease, with Brian scratching each pig's back whilst I passed the tape around the belly and noted the numbers. Our pigs, it seemed, were a good weight and on track.

Living where we do, we are very lucky to have the services of Ned, an excellent freelance slaughterman who works at the local abattoir, but who will come out to smallholdings in the area to kill pigs on-site. The fact that our pigs wouldn't have that awful journey to the abattoir was comforting for us, and when the time came we knew it would be a great comfort to the pigs too. As we didn't actually own a suitable mode of transport to get the pigs to the abattoir anyway, it was a winner all round.

Brian contacted Ned to book our pigs in and find out what was involved. Reassuringly, Ned agreed to come out and see the pigs in three or four weeks time, to judge the best slaughter date with us, as apparently Welsh White's often develop quicker than other pigs.

All this talk of slaughter brought it home to us that we had vastly over-estimated the amount of land our pigs would be able to turn over in the time they were with us. Although our pigs had done an excellent job on the patch we had given them, we had been naive in thinking that they would cover the whole field. Next time, we decided, we'd try giving them a smaller area and moving them to a new patch more frequently.

At 25 weeks the pigs were still just big kids; they 'd regularly play 'chase me' around their hut, and came bounding over to the fence whenever they saw us with a bucket, their little tails wagging like excited puppies.

Feeding time had actually become a two person job, by this stage. Each of us was responsible for feeding one pig...I pulled the short straw, of course, with mischievous Rob. Rob was particularly keen on his food and would try his best to nudge the bucket out of my hand before I had chance to tip the contents into the trough. We fed them some distance apart and tried to pour their food out at the same time, so as to avoid one finishing before the other. This way each pig had their fair share, and raids on each other's troughs were kept to a minimum.

~

June and July turned out to be hot and dry; it was so good to feel the sun on our backs at long last. It was lovely to enjoy being outside, instead of dodging inclement showers and gale-force winds. The heatwave however, did bring its own workload. We found that most jobs had to be completed either before breakfast or after dinner, since it was simply too hot to do them at any other time of the day! The pigs were feeling the heat too, and much of our time was spent creating a wallow for them, and keeping it constantly wet. The pigs loved sitting or lying in the wallow, coating themselves in mud that proved an effective sunscreen. Watching Rob and Chloe in the wallow, with snouts caked in mud, also provided us with an endless source of entertainment when it was too hot to do anything else. Up until now, on the few sunny days we'd had, we'd diligently spread Nivea's factor 30 on our pigs' ears, to help protect them; which of course caused much hilarity amongst the local farmers, who thought we'd gone soft in the head. The mud was a much better solution though, and negated the need to pursue the pigs around their pen, bottle hidden behind my back, as I tried to ambush the unwilling recipients who detested its fresh fragrance.

It was so dry, that by the beginning of July, many of the farmers were bemoaning the brown state of the pasture, and the mountain on the far side of the valley was flanked with patches of scorched fields. Enjoying the heat, chickens languished on their sides in the dust, legs stretched out and one wing raised to catch the sun's rays. Queues formed for the most popular dust-baths, and white chickens emerged grey and grubby, covered in a coating of fine loam. Racing to catch up with friends, clouds of dust issued from feathered rear-ends, like comic-book trails of exhaust fumes as the throttle let rip. And one evening, as I approached the coop on the hill to shut the girls away for the night, there was a loud thud followed by a large cloud of dust billowing from the doorway, which made me chortle as the image of an exploding chicken came to mind!

With the long dry spell predicted to continue until the end of the month at least, we decided to celebrate our Silver Wedding with a BBQ for the whole village. It would be an opportunity, we felt, to thank everyone for all the help they had given us since we'd arrived at Nantcoed, and plans were promptly set in motion.

The idyllic 'chilled out' days however, soon came to an abrupt halt, as, with several weeks of hot, dry weather still forecast, our borehole suddenly and without warning, ceased to work! As our only water supply, and with many thirsty mouths to quench, this was of huge concern. The tiny trickle of water in the stream made us wonder if our borehole had actually run dry, hard as this was to comprehend knowing the endless amount of rain we'd had previously. It was evening when we first discovered the problem; the toilet cistern refused to refill and the taps were completely dry. With the prospect of no morning cup of tea, or even enough water to clean our teeth with, we popped down to Rob and Chloe's in the village to fill up a couple of lemonade bottles that would see us through to the morning.

The thought that the borehole could be dry was very disturbing, and with very little water in the stream, even finding enough water for the animals was going to be a problem, let alone flushing toilets, washing and cooking. The prospect of possibly being without water for weeks was more than daunting, especially at a time when we had quite a lot of livestock to care for, and when they would need more water than usual with the heatwave in full swing.

We dug out all the information the previous owners had left us regarding the installation of the borehole. Studying all the documentation, it transpired that the pipe descended some 300ft, which, looking at the Ordnance Survey map, we calculated as being down to at least the same level as the river in the valley below. This settled it - the borehole couldn't be dry. We decided that the fault must be with the pump that brought the water to the house.

The following day, the news of our difficulties had reached most of the village, and we were inundated with offers of large containers and access to numerous private water supplies; it was a heart-warming response that we much appreciated in our frazzled state.

Suspecting now, that our problem was a mechanical one, we were soon on the phone to a local mother and son team of borehole specialists, who arrived within two hours to sort it out. Their knowledge was impressive, and they very quickly identified the problem...a blown socket in the ground, at the top of the borehole, which had not been sealed sufficiently when it was originally fitted. It had then blown the socket in the garage, where a compressor was housed, which pumped the water into the house. With the socket replaced, it was good to have the

161

water flowing again, and a massive relief. Having been totally ignorant of how our borehole system worked, it was reassuring to have a better understanding of such a vital piece of equipment, and it was good to know who we could call if there were further problems in the future.

~

July, we knew, would be a busy month, with fourteen ducks to pluck, my birthday and Sam's graduation all within 3 days of each other, not to mention a party to plan. However, very quickly further events were added to the social calendar, one of these being Elwyn's 70th birthday, a farmer who lived just across the valley from us. With the weather settled and sultry, a huge party for the whole village was planned, involving a bouncy slide, a pig roast, several barrels of beer and a live band.

Thankfully with so much to do, Sam returned home from uni a few days earlier than expected, and offered to help with the duck plucking. With more ducks in this batch than our last lot, we knew that getting them all plucked in a day would be impossible with just the two of us. We started at 9am and worked right through to 8.30pm, with very little in the way of breaks. By the time we had stacked all fourteen ducks in the freezer and consumed our well-deserved treat of fish and chips, none of us had the energy to move from our chairs. Our fingers and thumbs were sore and our backs ached.

The following day, being my birthday, saw us enjoying lunch overlooking the sea at New Quay. It was good to relax for a while, and enjoy the sunshine. With temperatures soaring into the low thirties, it was not the weather for anything too physical.

The next day we were 'suited and booted' for Sam's graduation in Swansea. With such high temperatures, formal suits, collars and ties, as well as academic gowns and mortar boards, would not be a recipe for comfort. Luckily, due to the exceptional conditions, a special dispensation was given to students, to remove their suit jackets for the ceremony. We fortunately, had plumped for taking most of our photos *before* the ceremony, when everyone was milling about in the foyer, ribbing each other about their graduate garb. By the time we all emerged from the building a couple of hours later, most students and guests appeared wilted and weary of posing for pictures. Exhausted by the occasion and the heat, we returned home, leaving Sam to party-on with his mates for the next couple of days.

With just one day to recover from the graduation, Saturday saw me starting a new job, cleaning holiday-lets; money was tight, so when the opportunity came my way I snapped it up. It was not really the best job to be doing in such humid conditions, and sweat dripped from me as I scrubbed and mopped. I returned home exhausted, ready to collapse into a chair with a cold drink. However, an emergency was in full flow as I walked through the door. It appeared that the clutch had gone on Sam's car as he was driving home, and that he'd managed to limp to the end of the M4 before it had died completely in the car park of a service station; could I go and tow him home? I grabbed the tow-rope and got straight back in the car.

By the time I reached Sam, about an hour later, he had decided that a rope would not be adequate for a tow of over 30 miles, and that we needed to drive back to Swansea to purchase a towing rod, which we did. Returning to the spot where we'd left Sam's car, we attempted to attach the rod to both cars. This proved more than tricky, with Sam's car only manoeuvrable by pushing; not easy when there are only two of you, and one of those needs to sit in the driver's seat and steer. Anyway, after a lot of muttered curses and sucking of air through clenched teeth, we finally had the two cars connected. As I pulled away, heart-wrenching clunks and bangs came from the connecting pole as the tension was taken up, and we tottered out onto the open road. After just a couple of hundred yards, I checked the rear-view mirror to find there was no sign of Sam or his car, and for a fraction of a second a wave of panic swept over me. I flicked my eyes across to the nearside wing mirror, and with relief saw the corner of his low-slung BMW edging out from behind my tail lights. With the spare wheel perched high on the boot of my RAV 4, and with the connection points of our two cars on opposite sides, Sam's car was being pulled along close to the grass verge, despite me driving close to the white lines in the centre of the road. We staggered along at no more than 30mph, 4-way flashers blinking, trying hard not to brake unduly or accelerate too quickly, clangs and bumps punishing each lapse in concentration. By the time we'd negotiated the series of busy roundabouts around Carmarthen, my nerves were utterly frayed, but on we pressed at our snail's pace. Eventually we reached the garage (which by now was closed) where we hoped to leave Sam's car to be fixed. I pulled it up the slope in front of the workshop doors and Sam uncoupled the towing bar. Leaving a note on the dashboard with our phone number, and saying we would be back first thing on Monday morning, we set off again relieved to have made it, but both of us shattered and our nerves in tatters.

We must have looked as bad as we felt as we arrived home, because Brian insisted that we have a strong cup of tea before venturing out to Elwyn's 70th party. None of us could muster enough energy for the bouncy slide, but it was a great night, chatting to our friends and listening to the live band. After a couple of hours we crept away, leaving the rest of the village partying well into the night. Tales of over-enthusiastic descents from the top of the inflatable giant slide (very possibly fuelled by a beer or two) were recounted in the shop for days, and the resultant sores and bruises were compared like prized trophies for weeks to follow.

First thing on Monday morning Sam and I returned to the garage where we'd abandoned his car on the forecourt. Luckily, they were fine about it all and agreed to fix the clutch. Sam made arrangements to pick his car up at the end of the week, and with that sorted we tackled the next problem. Sam needed to be in Herefordshire for the afternoon shift at a petrol station where he had a holiday job; being over 2½ hours away, the plan was for him to stay with his older brother. Without a working car, of course, Sam was unable to get there, so I set off on the five hour round trip to deliver him.

Feeling weary from recent events, and with our Silver Wedding party to organise in just five days, I felt as if I was wading through treacle as I tried to make preparations. However, when the day of the party arrived, drinks, alcoholic and non-alcoholic, were stacked in the kitchen, including three barrels of beer generously donated by Elwyn (remnants from his party the previous weekend) and food was prepared. Our friend, Phil, brought his 'all singing, all dancing' barbecue and set it up in the garage, offering to flip burgers in return for a steady flow of lager. John and Julie provided us with their gazebo, as predictably the forecast was for the heatwave to finally break into heavy showers during the evening, and family arrived from far afield, some staying with us and others booked in for Bed and Breakfast at Elwyn's farm across the valley.

Of course, true to form, at exactly 4pm the first drop of rain fell on Nantcoed, just as the first guests arrived carrying copious plates of delicious offerings for the table. However, the people of Felinfawr are not ones for ditching a party just for the sake of a bit of rain, and people happily perched beneath the makeshift tarpaulins and gazebos we'd rigged up on the patio for the night, in case of just such an occurrence. As the rain fast became a deluge, guests deftly manoeuvred their seats, so as to avoid the inevitable drips and splashes that found their way through the plastic sheeting. The bravest guests, with cagoules held high over heads or wrapped around shoulders, dashed between the garage and the kitchen, replenishing plates and glasses. It certainly wasn't the sultry summer's evening in the garden that we'd envisaged when we'd invited the whole village to join us in our small abode. However, it was a great evening, with around fifty of us partying well into the night. It lifted our hearts to see how many wonderful friends we'd made in the short time we'd lived in Felinfawr. We loved the strong community of Welsh and English that we now belonged to, and which had readily supported us in everything we'd done since taking on our smallholding. This was a community full of wonderful characters, who not only were quick to lend a helping hand, but whose mix of eccentricities invariably made every get-together a highly entertaining experience.

One such character was Nerys, a well-respected pillar of the farming community in her seventies, with a very dry sense of humour. On hearing that we proposed to keep geese she had solemnly recounted how she'd once reversed straight over one poor goose on the yard. The gander had apparently witnessed his mate's demise and for years had vociferously attacked her car whenever he saw her behind the wheel, pinning her there and refusing to let her out.

As our party drew to a close and some of our guests started to wend their way home, I spotted Nerys and her friend, Olwen, in the boot room. They had been there for quite some time, so I went to find out what the problem was. Nerys, it turned out, was having some difficulty finding her coat amongst the many that were hanging there. Establishing that it was black, we soon had it whittled down to just two choices, but Nerys still was undecided, unable to recall what hers looked like.

'Well it was new, you see', she explained in her broad Welsh drawl, 'And I wore it for the first time tonight.'

I asked her if I should enquire of the other guests if the coat she thought *might* be hers, belonged to any of them. That way, if nobody claimed it, it really must be hers.

Nobody did claim it and so she tried it on again.

'It doesn't fit as well as it did when I arrived,' she commented, plunging her hands into the pockets and swinging to left and right.

'I do think it's yours,' Olwen offered helpfully, 'Because I admired it when you came to pick me up.'

Finally resigned, though not wholly convinced, Nerys said her farewells, and the two made their way down the drive to Nerys' car, marvelling as they went at the coat's many wonderful, and previously overlooked, design features.

19.   P-Day

Mid-August saw the arrival of the day that Brian and I had in many ways been dreading...P Day (Pig Day, or more accurately, the day we slaughtered our pigs). Ned, from the abattoir, had been to look at the pigs a month or so before, to help us judge when they would be ready, and a date for his return was ringed on the calendar. We gathered ourselves together and put on a brave face; hard as we'd tried not to become attached to our pigs, we had developed a real fondness for the playful duo. However, the day before Ned was due, we had a call to say that he now had a funeral to go to and wouldn't be able to make it after all. With visitors arriving in a few days, we were forced to postpone 'the deed' until the beginning of the following week, and our pigs were given a brief reprieve. This proved most opportune, as it turned out, since the ice-cream freezer at the village shop chose this very moment to cease working. With a whole freezer standing empty in readiness for storing our pork, we were luckily able to step in and help.

The following week, with the ice-cream safely returned to the shop's new freezer, Ned was back, this time with his Burco boiler and some very sharp knives. We also had our own tea-urn ready and plugged in, as we were told that the process would require a great deal of hot water. Eric, who had shared the cost of the pigs with us, and who was having one of the pigs for his freezer, also arrived to help. As we waited for the Burco to boil, we chatted and ran through the plan of action. Brian had already parked his truck at the bottom of the field, so we could use it to carry the carcasses up to the garage for processing. All was going well, until someone realised that the lights on both boilers were no longer lit, and it transpired that we'd lost all power. Without power, of course, we had no water either - a major setback that threatened to scupper the whole day.

Brian got straight onto the phone and spoke to the electrician who lived in the village, and who'd helped us out with a few jobs when we'd first moved into Nantcoed. As luck would have it, he was just across the valley at one of the farms on the mountainside, chatting and generally putting the world to rights. Even more amazing - he actually had a mobile signal (something almost as rare as hen's teeth in Felinfawr). He was thankfully with us within minutes, and mending the fuse that had blown as a result of overloading the sockets with two hefty boilers. He persuaded us that we needed to replace the very old fuse-box and increase the power capacity to the garage, so as to avoid similar problems in the future, and arrangements were made for him to return a few days later.

With everything back on track, and the two boilers now hot, we were ready for the moment we'd been dreading. The hardest part of the plan was getting the boar into the pig house, so that we could protect him from seeing what was happening to his sister. Even with a bucket of feed and with him having had no breakfast, he was reluctant to go along with the plan, but Eric and I eventually coaxed him through the door, and quickly roped a wooden pallet across the opening to prevent his escape. However, our captive soon finished the pellets and turned his mind to getting his snout under the sides of the hut, in an effort to tip it over and make a bid for freedom. Eric and I leant our full weight on the roof and hoped it would be enough to counteract the immense strength of the large boar. Meanwhile Brian was feeding Chloe in her usual spot by the gate and she was completely oblivious to what Ned was doing. He scratched her head to soothe her and lined up the stun gun between her ears. One minute she was eating, the next she was dead. She knew nothing about it...a perfect way for her to go.

Lifting Chloe into the back of the truck, at an estimated dead weight of 100kg, took every ounce of effort that could be mustered, and I was briefly left to pin the hut down alone as Eric was called across to help. As she was driven up to the garage I released Rob from the hut. Remarkably, he seemed unperturbed by the absence of Chloe, and was just glad to be able to root about in the run again, looking for any tasty morsels that might have been missed earlier.

A wheel barrow helped us to get Chloe from the back of the truck to the garage, and all four of us lifted her onto a sturdy table, where the amazing process of butchering began. Firstly, the bristles were removed from the skin using the bottom of a candlestick; an amazing and ancient technique that did a really efficient job. Very hot water was poured onto the skin, and the candlestick moved in a circular action. The base of the candlestick was ideal, as it had an edge, but not a sharp edge that would tear the skin.

Once the skin was cleaned and prepared it was all hands on deck again, to hoist the pig into the air and tie it onto the rafters in the garage, so it could hang upside down for the next stage; the evisceration of the internal organs. Ned inspected the liver closely for white spots, which would indicate worm infestation, but thankfully it was completely clear and pronounced fit for human consumption.

Once both pigs were hanging in the garage, the clean-up operation could be mounted. With everyone doing their bit, this didn't take very long at all. The table, now clear of pigs, was bleached and scrubbed ready for the following day, when Ned would return to complete the job. The garage door was closed to keep out unwanted visitors (namely the cat), and we retired for a well deserved cup of tea and a glass of wine. Ned had been very impressed with the carcasses, which he regarded as having just the right amount of fat and a good proportion of meat. We were feeling 'well-chuffed' with ourselves, and pleased to have got the worst over with.

The next day Ned was back and an expectant crowd of four gathered by the garage doors. Eric's wife, Chrissie, and I were armed with abundant supplies of freezer bags, and the kitchen scales were poised to record the precise extent of our success at raising our own pork. A red kite circled overhead, sensing a possible meal, and Ned mused how they seemed to know his car and followed him everywhere.

As Ned sharpened his knives and began the task of jointing the carcasses, we were all entranced by his skill and knowledge. It was fascinating to learn where each cut of meat came from, and he bombarded Chrissie and myself with endless choices to be made as to the joints we each wanted. It was an intense process and quite wearing for the old brain! Brian and I decided that we'd like to cure some hams for Christmas and also to try curing some streaky bacon. There were shoulder and leg joints of various sizes, and 28 chunky chops to be bagged too. The rest of the meat on our pig was destined for sausages, which Ned would make and deliver back to us in a few days. Eric and Chrissie wanted cuts of belly pork and spare ribs, as well as some joints, but no sausages or hams. It was interesting to see how the butchering of each pig varied in order to cater for our different needs, and we all marvelled at the speed and skill employed by Ned. There was very little wasted. Our pig's head, which we didn't want, was gratefully received by a neighbour, who was looking forward to turning it into brawn; not something any of us novices felt we could remotely entertain or stomach.

Weighing all the meat from our pig, before we froze it, we were amazed to find that the grand total came to over 62kg! Comparing the equivalent cuts and prices of very ordinary Supermarket pork (not outdoor reared or organic) a huge saving was revealed. Our pig had only cost us £159.24 to buy, raise, kill and butcher, which was just a third of the retail price we'd have had to pay in the supermarket for what we considered to be an inferior product. The pigs had proved a real success on every level. We had learnt a great deal, and would no doubt adjust a few things the next time, but we were definitely convinced it was something we'd be doing again.

Whilst we'd been franticly bagging up of the joints and chops, we had become acutely aware of five new arrivals on our field, though we'd not had an opportunity at the time to investigate further. With the meat now safely stored in the freezer, the garage returned to being a garage again and everyone gone, we were able to turn our attention to the intruders.

Five dishevelled looking sheep eyed us warily from where they grazed on the top field, close to the chicken run. Hoping it was just a matter of ejecting the visitors back through a gap in the boundary fence, we inspected the wire netting thoroughly for holes, but the search proved fruitless. The only conclusion we could come up with was that they had either managed to jump over the fence from the field above us, or possibly more likely, had come in from the road, squeezing past the cars on the drive, when we were all busy in the garage. However they'd got there, we knew from past experience that sheep were bad news in relation to our electric fences, and if panicked could flatten or rip the netting, not to mention snap the plastic posts. As we had planned to be away the following day, visiting family in Herefordshire, and could not afford to leave our chickens unprotected by their fences during our absence, we were keen to resolve the problem quickly.

We decided to coax the sheep towards the gate on the bottom field, where we hoped to persuade them along the road to the next gate and back into their own field. However, with no sheepdog and only the two of us to implement this manoeuvre, we were doomed to failure from the start. The sheep were unconvinced by plan, and each time we thought we had them going in the right direction, they doubled back, running straight between us. Repeatedly we returned to square one and tried again, until finally, we surrendered and rang Dewi to let him know that we had a problem with some of his sheep. Unfortunately, Dewi wasn't there, so all we could do was to leave a message for him, asking him to give us a call as soon as possible.

With an early start planned for the morning, it was shortly after10pm that we climbed the stairs to bed, just as the phone rang. It was Dewi, and he said he would be right over! We were taken aback. Dewi had never been this quick off the mark when we'd had his sheep stray into our garden before. How, we wondered, was he going to extract the sheep in the dark, and without twisting his ankle on the treacherously uneven ground? But before too long Dewi arrived, torch in hand, and we were once again engaged in futilely chasing sheep, staggering uphill and careering downhill for well over an hour. Dewi called 'hup, hup', encouraging the sheep to come to him, but they were having none of it. Indeed they appeared to totally disregard his commands and promptly made for the highest and most inaccessible spot on the smallholding, behind the largest and thickest patch of brambles they could find. It was at this point we all admitted defeat and returned to the house. Dewi left, somewhat confused and more than a little stung by the disrespect his sheep had shown towards his authority. He promised to return the next day with 'one of the lads' and get it sorted, and we crawled into bed exhausted.

The following day we left early to visit friends and family. It was almost 6pm before we returned, weary from our day on the road, but on pulling into the drive we decided we should check on the sheep situation. We carefully scanned the field and were relieved to see that the sheep had gone. Dewi, we presumed, had finally rounded them up and returned them to his field. We retired to the house, unwrapped the fish and chips we'd collected on our way through town and put our feet up.

The phone rang shortly afterwards. It was Dewi.

'I see you got the sheep out,' I said. 'Thank you so much.'

'Well, actually they weren't mine,' Dewi replied. 'There were three lambs amongst them, and I don't have any lambs left. One had an ear tag and we tried to get them into a pen across the road so we could find out who they belonged to, but they ran off down the road, so I've no idea whose sheep they are.'

Poor Dewi, he'd spent so much time chasing them, the night before and much of the following morning, and then they'd turned out not even to be his sheep! We apologised profusely.

However, when we met up with Dewi and his wife a few days later at an after-wedding party in the village, we couldn't help but chuckle. Dewi's wife and sons, it appeared, had given him a great deal of ribbing about his blunder. His needless night-time pursuit and subsequent bungled day-time gathering, of five sheep that showed him absolutely no respect, and who he'd only belatedly recognised as not even being his, had sparked huge hilarity. And as we all relived the absurdity of the goings-on, fuelled by a good deal of alcohol, we were soon utterly helpless with laughter.

20. Completing the Harvest

A favourite spot for our morning cup of coffee, was on the veranda of the chalet, where we could survey our fields and the valley beyond. As we sat, chickens would wander purposefully amongst the tussocks, and we'd chortle at the random logic and complete absence of commonsense that our girls displayed. Invariably, we'd watch one chicken come across a tasty beetle or piece of apple and immediately pick it up and run about excitedly. This of course would attract the attention of all the others, who would then pursue her relentlessly until, inevitably, the prize was snatched away. Time and again the chicken whose find it initially was, fell into the same trap, but yet they persisted in this behaviour and seemed totally oblivious to the benefits of keeping the find hush-hush. A further anomaly (though to be fair this was probably beyond their control) was the annual moult that started just as summer ended and the chilly north wind first made an appearance.

After a beautiful start to the month, we were plunged into a bitterly cold snap for a couple of days, and, true to form, in the youngsters' run an explosion of feathers littered the ground, as if one of the girls had sneezed and dropped her full attire in one fell swoop. It was clear that someone was going to be subject to some dreadful draughts, being more than a few feathers short of the full set, though the unfortunate victim was, surprisingly, not immediately apparent.

Just a couple of weeks later however, all the chickens seemed to be at one stage or another of undress, and there was a distinct lack of eggs to be had. Some seemed to have very few feathers left at all, but the emergence of fresh new quills gave them a certain porcupine quality. Others just looked tatty with several feathers awry, in a sort of 'pulled through the hedge backwards' look, whilst some appeared to have donned a feather mini-skirt, with extra long legs and a small garter of feathers at the knee, marking their previous hemline. One poor girl even appeared to have had a 'Brazilian', losing all the feathers on her rear end in a perfect circle; one just didn't know where to look!

As autumn approached, our five geese seemed to know that time was rapidly running out, if they were to leave a lasting impression, and the group spent much of their time harassing me as I went about the daily chores. I was regularly cornered by the compost heap as I emptied the kitchen scraps, and relentlessly pursued on each trip to and from the chicken runs, by outstretched wings and a cacophony of honking. Rather like those annoying gangs of boys at primary school, who spend the whole of playtime dashing up and down the length of the playground causing as much annoyance to others as possible, our geese were fast falling out of favour with everyone. Progress across the lawn for cat, dog, chicken or human required a wary eye on the troublemakers' location at all times, and just as with our previous geese, this group were proving deviously cunning and persistently intimidating. When G-Day finally arrived, you could almost hear the entire smallholding breathe a sigh of relief.

Of course, it was now that Brian had to face the inevitability of his folly at insisting on having *five* geese. It was immediately clear that to pluck all five in one day would be simply impossible, and for once we would have to spread the job over two consecutive days. Thankfully, as we completed the final bird, our thumbs sore and throbbing, Brian adamantly announced that he was never ever going to raise more than *two* geese in future.

With the geese plucked, another year's harvest was complete. The freezers were full (all three of them) and at last it was safe to cross the garden without being frisked or threatened. It was time to put our feet up by the fire and take a well-earned break. We'd achieved so much since arriving at Nantcoed, and proved to ourselves that we could indeed raise most of our own meat and vegetables economically, on just three acres of poor quality land. Not only that, but our animals could live happy care-free lives, and meet their end with the minimum of stress. We had also taken strides to improve the land, and felt we'd started to make a difference, despite a lack of machinery and having to do everything laboriously by hand.

Over the winter decisions would be made about our next steps: the vegetables we'd grow, and the animals we'd rear for the table. The new year would bring new challenges, the long awaited asparagus bed might finally have enough seaweed to be planted, ducks no doubt would be raised, pigs too, and, maybe, just maybe, we'd give geese a miss and try our hands at raising a few turkeys instead (hurray!)

Some things however, were certain: there would be plenty of gatherings in the village hall to see us through the dark nights of winter, a wealth of banter and good humour to sustain us and plenty of time to 'go with the flow'.

We lived a frugal life now and finances were often tight, but our new adventure had brought us so much more than we could have ever dreamed of. We had come to Felinfawr in search of a simple life, a challenge that Brian and I could tackle together, far from the stresses of the modern world and with ample time to 'stand and stare'*. It had not been easy, we'd certainly had our setbacks, but life was good; we ate like kings, were part of a truly incredible community and, best of all, we'd learnt to laugh again.

What is this life if, full of care,
We have no time to stand and stare.
No time to stand beneath the boughs
And stare as long as sheep or cows.
No time to see, when woods we pass,
Where squirrels hide their nuts in grass.
No time to see, in broad daylight,
Streams full of stars, like skies at night.
No time to turn at Beauty's glance,
And watch her feet, how they can dance.
No time to wait till her mouth can
Enrich that smile her eyes began.
A poor life this if, full of care,
We have no time to stand and stare.

by William Henry Davies*

177

Acknowledgements

I would like to thank our two boys, without whose encouragement this book would probably never have been written, and without whose support and muscle many jobs on the smallholding would have been so much harder, if not impossible!

Printed in Poland
by Amazon Fulfillment
Poland Sp. z o.o., Wrocław